RUGBY, TENNESSEE

RUGBY, TENNESSEE

SOME ACCOUNT OF THE SETTLEMENT FOUNDED
ON THE CUMBERLAND PLATEAU

Thomas Hughes

Introduction by Benita J. Howell

The University of Tennessee Press / Knoxville

Copyright © 2008 by The University of Tennessee Press / Knoxville.
All Rights Reserved. Manufactured in the United States of America.
First Edition.

Originally published in London, 1881, under the title, RUGBY, TENNES-
SEE BEING SOME ACCOUNT OF THE SETTLEMENT FOUNDED ON THE CUM-
BERLAND PLATEAU BY THE BOARD OF AID TO LAND OWNERSHIP, LIMITED
A COMPANY INCORPORATED IN ENGLAND, AND AUTHORISED TO HOLD AND
DEAL IN LAND BY ACT OF THE LEGISLATURE OF THE STATE OF TENNESSEE.

Frontispiece: Thomas Hughes. Courtesy Historic Rugby Archives

This book is printed on acid-free paper.

Library of Congress Cataloging-in-Publication Data

Hughes, Thomas, 1822–1896.
    Rugby, Tennessee : some account of the settlement founded on
the Cumberland Plateau / Thomas Hughes ; introduction by Benita J.
Howell. —1st ed.
        p. cm.
    "Originally published in London, 1881"—T.p. verso.
    ISBN-13: 978-1-57233-611-7 (pbk.)
    ISBN-10: 1-57233-611-0 (pbk.)
    1. Rugby (Tenn.)—History.
    2. Collective settlements—Tennessee—Rugby—History.
    3. Utopias—Tennessee.
    I. Title.
    F444.R9H8 2008
    976.8'74—dc22   2007027207

"There need be no hesitation in affirming that colonisation in the present state of the world is the very best affair of business in which the capital of an old and wealthy country can possibly engage."—JOHN STUART MILL.

"Is it possible that I, who get indefinite quantities of sugar-hominy, cotton, buckets, crockery ware, and letter paper, by simply signing my name once in three months to a cheque in favour of John Smith and Co., traders, get the fair share of exercise to my faculties by that act, which nature intended for me in making all these far-fetched matters important to my comfort? It is John Smith himself, and his carriers, and dealers, and manufacturers; it is the sailor, the hide-dresser, the butcher, the negro, the hunter, and the planter, who have intercepted the sugar of the sugar and the cotton of the cotton. They have got the education, I only the commodity. This were all very well if I were necessarily absent, being detained by work of my own, like theirs, work of the same faculties, then should I be sure of my hands and my feet; but now I feel some shame before my wood-chopper, my ploughman, and my cook, for they have some sort of self-sufficiency, they can contrive without my aid to bring the day and year round, but I depend on them, and have not earned by use a right to my arms and feet."—R. W. EMERSON.

CONTENTS

Part III. Board of Aid to Land Ownership.
The Town Site of Rugby

INTRODUCTION

BENITA J. HOWELL

Thomas Hughes published *Rugby, Tennessee* to answer the most frequently asked questions about his American colonization project: What had prompted the well-known author to sponsor the settlement, and what were its aims? Was the Cumberland Plateau an auspicious setting, and would its people welcome the colony? What could prospective colonists expect of daily life in Rugby? The resulting volume is a primary document that offers much of interest beyond Hughes's prospectus for his colony in Morgan County, Tennessee.

Part I describes the plight of England's "Will Wimbles," the underemployed second sons of the gentry whom Hughes hoped to give a fresh start in Rugby. Here Hughes presents a cogent analysis of British political economy—the condition of the gentry, the middle-class tradesmen, and the working-class craftsmen and farmers as each experienced the transformation from an agrarian to an industrial society and the economic depression of the 1870s. Hughes felt that mercenary competition among tradesmen resulted in shoddy goods, dishonest advertising, and shady dealings, while the productive capacity and self-sufficiency of craftsmen and farmers was not only the essential base of a healthy economy but also ennobling for those workers. These chapters suggest why

Hughes espoused the principles of Christian Socialism, the cooperative movement, and workingmen's colleges. Only when he realized that the reforms he envisioned were unlikely at home did Hughes focus his energies on emigration and a colony where public school graduates would combine a livelihood gained through agricultural or other productive enterprises with the social and intellectual pursuits of gentlemen. Anyone interested in nineteenth-century social history will find in these chapters a highly readable account of Christian Socialist principles and Hughes's rationale for emigration.

Part II introduces the Cumberland Plateau, a little-known section of Tennessee that was just becoming connected to the outside world by a new railroad; it attracted additional public curiosity because of Hughes's decision to establish his colony there. The chapters in Part II first appeared in *The Spectator* in September and October of 1880, permitting readers to share vicariously in Hughes's first visit to Tennessee (and helping to finance his travel).[1] Development of the colony site and initial construction had been planned and supervised by Hughes's American associates and by the London Board's representative, John Boyle. Hughes himself first laid eyes on the plateau and the town site that he would name Rugby just a month prior to the official opening day, which he describes in the last of these sketches.

Hughes's aspirations for the Rugby colony are the theme of Part III, which resembles typical promotional literature for the many new settlements in the southern and western states in the 1870s and 1880s. This part begins with Hughes's address to the colonists, dignitaries, and local bystanders who assembled for opening day ceremonies on October 5, 1880. It continues with "Latest Views," an essay reprinted from the February 1881 *Macmillan's Magazine,* an update on accomplishments of the first few months. In an address given at Rugby School in April 1881 and reprinted as the third chapter, Hughes invited students at his *alma mater* to become colonists, quoting extensively from letters of two public school graduates sent from Rugby. Their descriptions of daily work routines were included in this address to counter impressions conveyed by the popular press that the colonists were devoted to "lawn tennis, and bathing and shooting parties" (134) rather than the hard work needed to establish homes in a wilderness.[2] Chapter IV continues the theme of colonist recruitment by excerpting information on soil, potential crops, and opportunities for manufactures from a report prepared by Col. J. B. Killebrew, secretary of the Tennessee Bureau of Agriculture, Statistics, and Mines.[3] He was well versed in geology and was frank about Cumberland Plateau soils and their limited agricultural potential. A glossary of facts useful to potential colonists concludes the volume.

The Rugby colony garnered a great deal of attention and media coverage in Britain and America because of its association with Thomas Hughes, whose best-selling novel, *Tom Brown's School Days* (1857), had catapulted him to fame on both sides of the Atlantic. Who was Thomas Hughes? What forces shaped his life and brought him to Tennessee?[4]

Hughes was born in Berkshire in the village of Uffington on October 20, 1822, where three generations of his grandmother's ancestors and his grandfather Thomas Hughes all had been vicars of the parish church. Grandmother Mary Ann Watts Hughes endowed

young Tom with great affection for Uffington and introduced him to literary acquaintances when Tom visited
her London home. One of these luminaries, Sir Walter
Scott, became Tom's favorite author, inspired his love of
poetry and fiction, and reinforced enthusiasms for local
history and folklore that the boy absorbed along with
his grandparents' stories of Uffington village and Berkshire's White Horse.

Tom's father, John Hughes, an only son, was a district
magistrate who was very active during the early 1830s
dealing with unrest and violent protest among agricultural workers. Witnessing these troubles began to shape
Tom's critique of the English class system and disposed
him to sympathize with the Chartists, workers who pre-
sented a People's Charter calling for greater attention to
their interests in Parliament, where the working class
had no elected representatives. Late in life, Hughes rec-
ollected his father's role: "My father was the most active
magistrate in the district. . . . He was an old fashioned
Tory, but with true popular sympathies, and had played
cricket and football all his life with the men and boys of
our village, and it is one of my proudest memories that
only one man from Uffington joined the rioters, and he
came back after three weeks ashamed and penitent."[5]

Biographers Mack and Armytage observe that
Hughes greatly admired his father's model of the pater-
nalistic country squire who was attached to his land and
solicitous for the welfare of the people who worked it.
He became increasingly nostalgic for a rural social order
that seemed to be passing from the scene. Trade and
manufacturing dominated the British economy of the
late nineteenth century, but these were not considered
socially acceptable occupations for younger sons of the

landed gentry. At the same time, the very success of public schools such as Rugby had produced an over-supply of gentlemen graduates seeking socially approved positions as military officers, clergymen, lawyers, or men of letters. Hughes felt keenly that idleness and dependence on allowances from family was demoralizing to these young men and a shameful waste of their potential. The Rugby colony proposed a new start that would blend hard work and respect for ordinary manual labor with the accustomed social and intellectual pursuits of gentlefolk.

Hughes's concerns encompassed much more than the social and economic change that seemed to be making his class superfluous in British society, however. He sensed that the mercenary spirit of Britain's ascendant merchant and industrialist middle class threatened the traditional moral order of the rural gentry. Along with the traditional values of *noblesse oblige* that he had observed in his father, during his years at Rugby School under the guidance of headmaster Thomas Arnold, Hughes had developed a strong sense of Christian obligation to struggle for just treatment of all people. Hughes hoped that his colony in rural America would offer gainful employment and livelihood to second sons of the British gentry, but more important was his hope that this new agrarian community could be a respite from the constant competition and preoccupation with wealth that pervaded Britain. His chief desire was that Rugby should become a place where young public school graduates could live out the values that Rugby and other progressive public schools taught.

In many respects, the plan for Rugby was an outgrowth of Hughes's participation in the Christian Socialist movement inspired by clergyman Frederick Denison

Maurice.[6] Following his graduation from Oxford, Hughes began reading law at Lincoln's Inn, London, in 1845. There he encountered John Malcolm Ludlow, a politically aware young lawyer, who invited Maurice to conduct chapel services at Lincoln's Inn. Maurice and Ludlow along with clergyman Charles Kingsley formed the core of the Christian Socialist movement. When Maurice first proposed that Hughes should join the group, the others dismissed him as a good soul but an athlete rather than someone who could aid their central project of education. In fact, Hughes became a key participant in several ways. First, in his periodical contributions, he was able to articulate Maurice's message clearly, translating abstract principles into substantive terms. For example, when Maurice inaugurated a series of "Tracts on Christian Socialism" with *Dialogue between Somebody (a Person of Respectability) and Nobody (the Writer)*, Hughes immediately followed with a readable *History of the Working Tailors' Association* (1850) that illustrated the application of Christian Socialist principles and set forth Hughes's own beliefs in much the same manner as Part I of *Rugby, Tennessee*.[7]

Second, whereas Maurice was content to preach the philosophy of Christian Socialism, Hughes constantly urged him translate these principles into concrete action: tangible support for the cooperative movement and a school to implement the group's belief that education was the means through which the working classes could better themselves. In 1850, Hughes became key organizer of the Council of Promoters within the Society for Promoting Working Men's Associations, a vehicle through which the Christian Socialists would provide practical legal and political assistance to trade unions.

Later Hughes's call to action was heeded when the Christian Socialist core group established the London Working Men's College in 1854. Hughes himself commented: "I am not much of a thinker or projector. . . . I think it is more fit that I should take my full whack as executor."[8] Correspondence reveals that Hughes played a vital role in making a team out of a group of strong and sometimes eccentric personalities, "recruits from every walk of life: a scholar, a politician, a doctor, an architect, a poet, a critic, a couple of publishers, and five working class men. His good will and tolerance held them together; others came up with ideas for projects while Hughes was vigorous in doing the work and in bringing in other old Rugby school graduates to help."[9]

From his earliest association with the Christian Socialists, Hughes had been politically active in support of trade unions. The Society for Promoting Working Men's Associations organized in 1850 and supported the Working Tailors' Association and other such unions. Kingsley (and the other Christian Socialists) believed that workers should "associate for work instead of for strikes."[10] Hughes provided legal advice to newly established unions and encouraged them to function as producer cooperatives. Along with Maurice and Ludlow, he hoped to foster an alliance of producer and consumer cooperatives and in the process to bridge the long-established class distinctions that separated workers from middle-class consumers. Hughes helped the unions attain recognition as legal entities through his lobbying for passage of the Industrial and Provident Societies Act in 1852. The National Cooperative Congress held in the summer of 1852 was the climax of Christian Socialist involvement in the cooperative movement, however. Soon thereafter consumer cooperatives began to dominate the movement and workers withdrew from the Cooperative League. E. V. Neale, secularist champion of consumer cooperatives, and Christian Socialist Ludlow came to loggerheads, but Hughes continued to work with both of them and encourage reconciliation of their differences until the late 1870s, when he reluctantly concluded that the Cooperative Congress was concerned chiefly with saving consumers money rather than applying Christian principles to business.[11]

Hughes had invested money as well as time to assist some of the nascent trade unions of the 1850s, and when they disintegrated because of financial mismanagement he lost money. This was the first but not the last instance in which Hughes backed his political enthusiasms with investments that cost him financially. Yet this setback for worker organizations strengthened the Christian Socialists' interest in better preparing workers for self-governance through education. In his travels to provide legal advice to trade unions, Hughes had an opportunity to observe the People's College in Sheffield that the Chartists had established; he became a key promoter of the London Working Men's College, based on the Sheffield model but offering liberal studies as well as technical courses.

Mack and Armytage summarize the Christian Socialists' aspirations for the college as follows: "Its object was twofold. On the one hand, the wealthy were to be influenced by giving them contact with the poor; on the other, workers were to be trained to share the life of the nation, and so reform it from within."[12] Hughes deferred to others to teach academic subjects, but he took a role in admissions and organized extracurricular sport and social activities. He used his skill in boxing to gain the respect of burly, rough workers who initially were skeptical that the college had anything to offer them. Following his father's example, Hughes was able to use sport to overcome the inevitable distance between the middle-class Christian Socialists and the working men whom they sought to attract to the Working Men's College. Class distance prevailed between those teaching academic subjects and their students, but just as his father had done in Uffington, Hughes interacted on an equal footing with members of the cricket team and rowing club that he organized; all were respected equally for their athletic abilities regardless of social class. Some of this erasure of class distance also spilled over into the social evenings at the Working Men's College that Hughes arranged.

Hughes had published political essays and had served briefly as editor of the *Journal of Association,* but he never aspired to become a writer of fiction. His first and most successful work, *Tom Brown's School Days* (1857), was addressed to his eldest son, Maurice, when the eight-year-old was about to leave home for school in 1856. Hughes pondered the advice he wanted to give and hit upon a story as the most effective means of communicating it. Thus, without consciously setting out to do so, Hughes wrote and was persuaded to publish the first book for boys that spoke to them from their own perspective rather than preaching from an adult educator's point of view. Hughes's publisher, Alexander Macmillan, was a fellow Christian Socialist. *Tom Brown*'s immediate and lasting popularity astonished everyone, Hughes most of all. Ever after, the public identified Hughes with the obviously autobiographical protagonist Tom Brown.

The protagonist of his second novel, *The Scouring of the White Horse* (1858), is a materialistic London clerk who experiences a personal awakening during a vacation in Berkshire.[13] As Richard becomes absorbed in learning the traditions that link King Alfred to the ancient horse figure carved into the stone of White Horse Hill, he comes to appreciate rural life and the custom of the annual scouring that has preserved the horse figure. Richard's courtship of Lucy seems to bring out the best in him, much as Hughes's desire to win approval of their engagement from Frances Ford's parents had focused Tom on his studies during his final two years at Oxford.

Hughes's third novel, *Tom Brown at Oxford,* was serialized in *Macmillan's Magazine* before being published as a book in 1861. Like many sequels written because of popular demand, *Oxford* garnered less critical and popular acclaim than *School Days,* yet its diffuse structure encompasses many themes that reveal Hughes's reflections on his own experiences at Oriel College.

As a schoolboy, Tom Brown (and Tom Hughes at Rugby) had been shaped decisively by the master's ethical and social precepts, excelling in leadership and athletics rather than academics. When Tom Brown goes up to Oxford in the sequel, at first he is attracted to the "fast set," but before long he rejects both their snobbishness and their cavalier neglect of study. Hardy, a poor but gifted student who is working his way through college, counters Tom's attraction to the wastrels in the "fast set," whose attitudes and behavior Hardy abhors. Hardy in *Oxford* in some respects fills the role of Arthur in *School Days,* the studious boy who coached Tom in

lessons while Tom became his social mentor and pro-
tector from bullying, but Hardy also fills the master's
role as moral and spiritual mentor. He is the sounding
board as Tom Brown struggles with conflicting reactions to the Oxford Movement: attraction to its program
of self-denial and service to the poor but distaste for its
absorption in Anglo-Catholic ritual. In later life, Hughes
was an ardent supporter of the Church of England who
argued that proposals for its disestablishment would
cease only when the church reached out to incorporate
dissenters and non-conformists. He was convinced that
only a Broad Church not obsessed with ritual forms
could effect that reconciliation; Anglo-Catholicism alien-
ated non-elites and would undermine the church if left
unchecked.

Having published three novels in four years, Hughes
decided that he was not meant to be a professional nov-
elist. His only other piece of fiction was "The Ashen Fag-
got," a Christmas story published in 1862. He redirected
his energies to his legal practice and found a direct avenue for furthering his political beliefs by standing for
election to Parliament in 1865.

With the support and campaign contributions of workers, in the summer of 1865 Hughes was elected to the
House of Commons to represent the working-class Lambeth district of London; however, he took an independent stance that did not always coincide with workers'
agendas. He advocated expansion of the franchise and
sponsored bills to strengthen the rights of trade unions,
to limit work to a fifty-four hour week, and to improve
urban sanitation; on the other hand, he disapproved of
workers' opposition to mechanization and supported the

share-ownership scheme that coal mine owner Henry
Briggs introduced to avert strikes among his workers. In
his travels around the country to attend labor meetings,
Hughes did not hesitate to lecture workers on his views
of their best interests. Nor did his support for Sunday
closings, strict hours for sale of drink, and advocacy for
regulation of weights, measures, and quality of goods
sit well with the small shopkeepers and publicans of
his Lambeth constituency. In 1868 Hughes was elected
from a more rural district, the town of Frome in Som-
erset; by 1874 he had lost the support of his party and
was defeated by a wide margin in the general election.
Commenting on Hughes's years in Parliament, Mack and
Armytage conclude that he took up too many causes at
once and thus irritated his parliamentary colleagues
and accomplished less as an M.P. than he might have
done had he chosen his battles more carefully.[14]

Perhaps Hughes's most important contribution to
government during his years in Parliament was his service on the Trade Union Commission, a body that collected information prior to introducing new legisla-
tive measures. Hughes effectively countered efforts of
employers to redefine unions as illegal conspiracies.
He authored a minority report advocating that unions
should have the right to sue, to amass strike funds, and
to picket; however, in the end he supported a compromise
that called on both unions and capitalists to submit disputes to voluntary boards of arbitration. He later served
as a labor dispute arbitrator on several occasions.

Mack and Armytage perceptively sum up the com-
plexity of Hughes's position in explaining why the Briggs
scheme of employer-directed alliance between capital and labor appealed to him: "For years Hughes had

been trying to reconcile three ideas: his love of the common man; his feeling that perhaps workers were not quite ready to handle their own affairs; and his desire to save his own class from being considered useless or pernicious."[15] Hughes found it increasingly difficult to reconcile the world of London society, where he was very much at home, with the workers' organizations where his political sympathies lay. As he became more conciliatory in disputes between management and labor, militant labor leaders who had appreciated his past assistance shunned his further involvement in their affairs.

Hughes suffered repeated disappointments following his parliamentary defeat. Church authorities ignored his campaign for Broad Church reforms that would bring non-Conformists back into the fold. Increasingly secular, democratic leaders in the labor movement and the Cooperative Congress spurned Hughes's appeal to Christian principles to elide class differences and quell economic competition. Following Maurice's death in 1872, Hughes was named principal of the Working Men's College of London, but he became embroiled in defending Maurice's reputation in print against secular critics. In 1875, his friend and fellow Christian Socialist Charles Kingsley died; some of the cooperative enterprises that Hughes had supported failed; his brother Hastings went bankrupt; and Fanny Hughes suffered serious illness. Hughes's sister Jeannie, a kindred spirit who had ardently supported his social activist causes as well as encouraging his writing career, died in 1877.

At the end of the decade, Hughes considered campaigning to regain a seat in Parliament but got no encouragement from his party. He wrote to his American friend, James Lowell, "I doubt if I shall ever return to the

House as my views on the Church question make me an almost hopeless candidate in the North of England, and my support of co-operation a perfectly hopeless one at present in the South."[16]

After the disappointments of the 1870s, Hughes, ever the optimist, redirected all his energies into what he called "the last castle in Spain I am ever likely to build"— the Rugby colony (46). When Hughes realized that Christian Socialist reforms were unlikely to be implemented at home, he began to advise emigration as the best means for both workingmen and the Will Wimbles of the gentry to escape Britain's entrenched socioeconomic system and make a new start. He first leaned towards Canada as a destination, but the United States eventually won his allegiance because of personal friendships developed on both sides of the Atlantic. Chiefly responsible was the New England poet and political essayist James Russell Lowell.

Hughes discovered Lowell's poetry, and the two began exchanging letters in the 1850s. Hughes admired Lowell's plain speech, and Lowell found Hughes to be more open and less pretentious than the typical Briton. Hughes met many Unionist Americans who visited England with letters of introduction from Lowell. He supported abolition of slavery in political tracts and wrote the introduction to the English edition of Lowell's *Bigelow Papers* (1859).

While remaining officially neutral, the British government sought to protect the textile industry's relations with Southern cotton producers, but for Hughes nothing could condone slavery. He voiced his unpopular convictions courageously during the war, and afterwards he urged prompt resolution of reparation claims and other wartime grievances along with reconciliation between Britain and the United States.

In 1870, Hughes visited America for the first time as Lowell's guest, taking every opportunity in the cities where he was invited to speak to explain Britain's stance to Americans and foster cordial postwar Anglo-American relations. Tennessee and the South were not on Hughes's itinerary, but he visited Chicago and Omaha as well as New England and the Middle Atlantic and saw enough of the West to realize that America's sparsely settled lands held promise for colonization.

Rugby ended up in Tennessee rather than Texas (where Hughes's son had located) because Hughes joined forces with an American colonization scheme that already had chosen the Cumberland Plateau site.[17] When the financial depression of the 1870s created industrial layoffs in New England, Boston businessman Franklin Webster Smith proposed returning surplus industrial workers to agriculture, but in a more favorable environment than the rocky farms that they had left for urban factory work. In late 1877 Smith and like-minded Boston merchants and industrialists formed the Boston Board of Aid to Land Ownership and began seeking suitable locations for settlement in the western and southern states. By June of 1878 they had decided to acquire land in Scott and Morgan Counties, Tennessee, near the final link in the Cincinnati Southern Railway. Land speculators with insider knowledge as to the railroad's exact route had acquired options to buy nearby lands, and it was such options that Cyrus Clarke, a former short-line railroad executive from Pennsylvania, offered Smith's group. One Rugby oral tradition explained that A. L. Crawford, a Clarke business associate (in fact his primary creditor), overheard members of Smith's party discussing their land quest while sharing a train car with them; Crawford introduced himself and suggested that they look into Clarke's Tennessee lands. After gathering information and inspecting the area with Clarke, the Boston Board hired him as their land agent and general manager. By this time, however, the recession was ending, factories were hiring again, and many of Smith's New England subscribers had lost interest in his scheme. Thus Smith turned to Hughes and proposed a merger with his London Board.

Franklin W. Smith was an abolitionist and charter member of the Massachusetts Republican Party, and his leadership in establishing the Young Men's Christian Association in Boston (the first YMCA in America) closely paralleled Hughes's involvement with the London Working Men's College. Smith traveled widely, so he may have been among the Americans who sought out Hughes with a letter of introduction from Lowell, or they may have met during Hughes's 1870 visit to Boston; the two leaders and their respective Boards of Aid to Land Ownership clearly were connected through the Russell Sturgises, Junior and Senior. The younger Russell Sturgis, who was a key member of the Boston Board of Aid, had been Smith's friend since college days and his co-worker in establishing the Boston YMCA. His father, who was a principal investor in the London Board, had moved to London and become an executive in the Baring Bank following many years in the China Trade. Perhaps the merger proposal was communicated to Hughes through the Sturgises. At any rate, John Boyle traveled to Tennessee to inspect the site and made a favorable report to the London Board at the end of 1878, paving the way for merger of the Boston and London ventures early in 1879. The merged boards resolved to develop a joint Anglo-American colony "where cultivated persons of modest means could establish comfortable homes in a healthful country setting."[18]

Rugby languished in the early twentieth century; many structures deteriorated or burned, and timber clear-cutting threatened what remained; but beginning in 1966, historic preservation legislation encouraged Brian Stagg and Oscar Martin to organize restoration efforts.[19] In its daily tours, exhibits, and award-winning orientation film, the non-profit Historic Rugby organization tells the story of Rugby's nineteenth-century beginnings and the community's tenacity and revival in the twentieth century. Descendants of original colonists and their plateau neighbors, newcomers like the Martin family who discovered Rugby and then dedicated themselves to conserving it, and countless tourists and contemporary residents have fallen in love with the place and become engrossed in its history. *Rugby, Tennessee* satisfies newcomers' curiosity about Rugby's origins just as it answered the questions of prospective colonists in 1881. Even if Rugby had not survived to stimulate such interest in its beginnings, however, Hughes's travel sketches still would merit reprinting.

Hughes's observations are especially valuable because there are few extant nineteenth-century descriptions of the northeastern section of Tennessee's Cumberland Plateau, which was quite inaccessible prior to construction of the Cincinnati Southern Railway. Mark Twain caricatured Jamestown in Fentress County as "Obedstown" in *The Gilded Age,*[20] but his description was based on Clemens family stories rather than firsthand observation. In 1867, when John Muir passed through Jamestown and Montgomery in Morgan County, the devastation and guerilla violence of the Civil War years were still evident. A thief joined Muir and left him alone only after rummaging through his pack and finding nothing of value. After he had "passed the poor, rickety, thrice-dead village of Jamestown, an incredibly dreary place," Muir encountered a gang of ten guerillas on horseback but got past them because they mistook him for a poor herb doctor. He was well fed in an African American household that evening and the next morning passed the "shabby village" of Montgomery, the Morgan County seat, with no further comment.[21]

The travel sketches in *Rugby, Tennessee* are enjoyable not only because Hughes was a talented writer, adept at using concrete detail to help readers visualize people and places, but also because his genial personality predisposed him to encounter backwoods country and its inhabitants with an open mind. Having decided that his colonists would thrive best in rural surroundings, he was not inclined to focus, as many local colorists did, on backwoods barbarity in comparison with civilized urban life. He prefaced his observations on "The Natives" by distancing himself from writers who already were exploiting Appalachia for the entertainment of Northern readers: " . . . let me introduce you to our neighbours, so far as I have as yet the pleasure of their acquaintance. And I am glad at once to acknowledge that it *is* a pleasure, notwithstanding all the talk we have heard of 'mean whites,' 'poor white trash,' and the like, in novels, travels, and newspapers" (61).

Hughes described the poorest farms and commented on both white and African American laborers; but unlike many local colorists who only briefly passed through the regions they described and who encountered locals mostly in the course of seeking food and lodging, Hughes was guided by men who had been on site for several months helping to survey and establish the town. Through them he was introduced to and dined with the more prosperous local families. He met "natives" who had lived in the area since the 1830s and relative newcomers who had immigrated from the North shortly before or after the Civil War. In a few brief essays, Hughes suggested the diversity of the region's population prior to arrival of the Rugby colonists.

Hughes was a keen observer and inclined to be fair-minded, but he was writing to encourage prospective colonists. To what extent did that purpose introduce bias into his observations and commentary? To begin with the easiest assessment, anyone familiar with Rugby and its environs can attest to the accuracy of Hughes's descriptions of the physical environment. Much of the surrounding land is still covered in a scrub forest of pine and white oak, though sadly the chestnuts survive only as saplings and in place names. Woodpeckers, hawks, and owls are still the most noticeable birds in these woods, and along sunny roadways several varieties of goldenrod appear in spectacular displays of late summer wildflowers. Umbrella and bigleaf magnolias still grow in the stream gorges alongside towering *Rhododendron maximum,* and the moist entrances to rock shelters harbor an abundance of maidenhair and rarer ferns. Hikers will recognize landmarks such as the Gentlemen's Swimming Hole or Rock Castle Falls and Cudjo's Cave in Fentress County.[22]

Hughes praised the picturesque scenery as one would expect a cultivated British gentleman to do, but

his Opening Day address went further in admonishing
the colony to conserve these natural assets by preserv-
ing the most beautiful areas for public enjoyment. The
original town plan reflected the best principles of late
Victorian suburban landscape design, and Rugby's lan-
guishing during most of the twentieth century insured
minimal intrusion of discordant elements that would
have obscured that design or undermined contemporary conservation efforts that protect natural as well as
architectural resources.[23]

Hughes gathered his impressions of the Cumberland Plateau at an auspicious moment when East Tennessee was attracting Northerners with capital to invest.
Through numerous speeches and publications, individual citizens, local committees, and finally the state had
solicited immigration from the North, especially to East
Tennessee.[24] Judge Oliver P. Temple, who later advised
the Board of Aid on contested land claims, was a prominent New South advocate who had personally met with
Franklin Smith and associates and assured them that,
because of contributions Boston had sent to aid belea-
guered Unionists during the war, they would surely be
welcome in East Tennessee.[25]

The opportunity to contribute directly to a Northern effort toward reunification and economic revitaliza-
tion in a Southern state would have appealed greatly to
Hughes. His devotion to abolition of slavery and postwar
reconciliation certainly affected what he reported, if not
what he saw. Hughes traveled to the plateau on the new
Cincinnati Southern Railway only months after it had
been completed through Morgan County. He praised the
railroad as a feat of engineering that was transforming
the spirit of the region by opening it up to distant mar-

kets for its agricultural and industrial products (37–38). Following the lead of New South boosters,[26] he praised especially General John T. Wilder, who had returned to Chattanooga, reconciled with his former Confederate enemies, and established a thriving iron industry at the southern end of the Cumberland Plateau (66–67).

Once established in Rugby, however, Hughes realized that development was bringing problems as well as benefits. Whether laborers worked in one of the new industrial enterprises along the railroad or on construction projects in Rugby, cash in their pockets and Sundays off brought purveyors of moonshine and gamblers to the neighborhood. Twice Hughes commented that construction in Rugby had been slowed because native laborers had been unfit for work on Mondays following weekend sprees (50, 64). He confidently resolved to deal with the problem by setting a proper temperance example in Rugby; however, booths at some distance in the woods (blind tigers) and the many saloons in the nearby coal mining town of Glenmary continued to tempt not only the native workers but many a thirsty British immigrant as well.

Concerning race relations, Hughes certainly was overly optimistic in assessing the extent of social transformation in southern Kentucky, where he was "surprised, and, I need not say, greatly pleased, to see the apparently excellent terms on which the white and coloured people were consorting, even in the Kuklux regions through which we came" (39). Nevertheless, Hughes employed a conventional stereotype when he described the black urchins he saw along the tracks as "little figures of fun" (39). The Sambo stereotype made it possible for even such a reformer as Hughes to overlook the poverty and harsh conditions still imposed on African American railroad workers after Emancipation. In any case, Hughes repeated what he had been told, that few African Americans were living near Rugby. After spending more than a month in residence, Hughes corrected that impression in an essay on "The Negro 'Natives,'" in which he reported that African Americans were moving into the area in substantial numbers seeking work.

In comparison with the white natives, Negroes worked more consistently and were "much more obedient . . . and manageable" (79). Unlike local whites, Hughes implied, these workers refused to sell their votes and were strongly committed to educating their children. These characteristics promised a bright future for African Americans in the South, Hughes said, but he immediately suggested that domestic service was their natural place, as evidenced by the willing and good-natured Negro boy "Jeff," who competently took over when a white youngster balked at boot blacking and water hauling (78–84).

Present-day readers may find it difficult to reconcile the racist tone of Hughes's anecdotes with his staunch advocacy for the abolition of slavery; his stereotypic characterization of African Americans reflects how thoroughly racism permeated the thinking of Victorians on both sides of the Atlantic. The most prominent of the loyal Unionists of East Tennessee, whose presence there became the basis for recruiting Northern capital and new settlers to the region, had supported slavery while vehemently opposing Secession. Their leader, Parson William G. Brownlow, who had raged against both rebels and abolitionists in his *Knoxville Whig* newspaper, was elected governor in 1865.[27] Some East Tennesseans shared Hughes's abolitionist sentiments, but even their Christian benevolence was intertwined with paternalism; the mission to uplift the less fortunate only underscored fundamental assumptions of racial and class superiority.

Despite Hughes's initial intent to set aside local color stereotypes, colonialist assumptions ultimately shaped his assessment of "natives" and others living in the area. In the course of writing letters that first appeared in the *Spectator* over a period of two months, Hughes revealed perhaps more than he intended about the colonists' elitism and local reactions to colonization.

Among the first local people Hughes sketched was an industrious New England woman who operated an inn near Cudjo's Cave. She and her husband had lived through the Civil War in Jamestown.[28] Hughes reported that she "had nothing but good to say of her native neighbours, except that they could make nothing of the country. 'The Lord had done all he could for it,' she summed up, and 'Boston must take hold of the balance'" (58). An appeal to higher uses of land and greater development of resources is, of course, a typical rationale for colonialism. From this meeting with a fellow outsider who thus approved the Rugby scheme, Hughes turned to "The Natives."

Squire Isaac Riseden of Horseshoe Bend was the leading citizen of the section where the new town was located. Mrs. Riseden provided an abundance of excellent food when Hughes was their guest for dinner; the squire, a Union army veteran, was courteous, intelligent, and ready to converse on any subject. The Riseden farm was prosperous although "very slovenly" by English standards of farm management (62).

Many of the natives, however, were "quite content to live from hand to mouth" (63) in "log-huts and cabins which, at home, could scarcely be rivaled out of Ireland" (62). These poor families needed wage labor to survive, but the men were undependable workers. Bearing in mind that "The Cumberland Mountains" was first published in the September 1 *Spectator,* the next four sketches in the September 10 issue, and "Our Negro 'Natives'" in October, one sees that Hughes gradually developed a negative assessment of the poor whites he had resolved not to stereotype. In addition to the temptation of drink, Hughes blamed an inordinate love of hunting and trapping for the native laborers' slipshod farming and slacking on contract work. Readers of *Rugby, Tennessee,* will miss some of the irony in this assessment because Hughes omitted the first section of his September 10 letter to the *Spectator* from the book. In "The Luxury of Loafing" he had written:

> Almost every cottage or shanty, as they call these attractive wooden houses, has a deep verandah (from which you get a view, over the forest, of the southern range of mountains, with Pilot Knob for highest point), and, in the verandah, rocking-chairs and hammocks, in one or other of which a chatty host or hostess is almost sure to be found, enjoying air, view, rocking, and the indescribable depth of blue atmosphere which laps us all round. . . . Every now and again, a merry group of young folk go by in wagon or on horseback; but even they are loafers, as they have no object in view beyond enjoying one another's company, and possibly lunch or tea at the junction of the two mountain-streams. . . . Their parents . . . take their own ease in the verandahs or shady grounds of 'The Tabard.'"[29]

Was loafing to be a luxury exclusive to the newcomers? In Rugby the American leisure class and British gentlemen accustomed to expecting deference from well-trained domestic and personal servants encountered mountaineers who disdained subservience to anyone and held rigid ideas about appropriate gendered division of labor. Hughes made light when the young native employed to serve the two ladies and six men staying at Pioneer Cottage walked off the job (80), but the boy's reaction surely revealed cultural differences and resentments as much as personal foibles. Rugby's colonization scheme raised the stakes; outsiders were claiming land, setting the agenda for its development, and asserting cultural hegemony.

If Hughes personally encountered more serious local resistance during his visit to Rugby, he chose not to mention it in *Rugby, Tennessee,* for obvious reasons; however, the Board of Aid's representative John Boyle recounted his own experience in a letter to Judge Temple.

We have settled, I believe, beyond any further question or difficulty the purchase of the Thompkins [*sic*] lands. The Riseden ones are in process of arrangement for becoming ours. The same with Mr. Schenck for all that we really much want of his, this very morning, a small addition being obtained at an enhanced figure which composed a little unwillingness which existed. The Peters lands I believe we know how to get hold of. . . . The Massengale property was a week or so ago secured by Mr. Clarke, and the document signed by all the parties, on terms extremely favourable as to price. This evening, however, having been invited to visit the family, and proceeding to read, at their request the document once again, just as he turned the first page the old lady snatched the document from his hand and pocketing it said 'I'll keep this, I want to read it through (or look it through) again.' Mr. Clarke might, by keeping his hold, have torn it—but he preferred not to do this—and contented himself with pointing out the illegality of the act and letting her know that this proceeding would not interfere with the operation of the instrument whose contents were well known and would have to be acted upon, as a fairer document was never drawn up. . . .

This strange episode has made a sensation, but to keep it to ourselves, [we] are determined for the present to take no notice of it, their [*sic*] being an impression with some that they will speedily come to their senses and return the document. I am not sure that I share this confidence.[30]

Boyle's apprehension was well founded, for the Massengales retained possession of their farm on the outskirts of Rugby. Uncle Dempsey and Aunt Betty Massengale later became favorites of Rugby's young people, but they are absent from Hughes's sketches.

Who, in Hughes's estimation, would best be able to bridge the cultural divide between Cumberland Plateau natives and British and American gentlefolk? In "Our Forester," Hughes related at length the accomplishments of Amos Hill, son of a laborer on a Warwickshire estate. As a boy Amos had done odd jobs, worked in the estate's gardens and livery stable, and later become personal servant to a railroad contractor. When Hughes met him, Amos Hill was managing the gardens in which young men were supposed to apprentice and learn farming skills, and he had laid out and supervised building of the bridle paths into the Clear Fork gorge. Meanwhile Mr. Hill's wife and son were operating the family farm some distance away at Glades, raising improved breeds of hogs, sheep, and cattle, and managing a comfortable, well-appointed house.

As in his fiction writing, Hughes espoused praiseworthy moral traits through the words attributed to Amos Hill. As a boy young Amos had absorbed Lady Mary's Sunday school lessons along with learning his place and duties on the estate. His high spirits led him to escalate a running dispute between the railroad and gamekeepers until he had a scrape with the law over poaching; Amos and his wife had then decided to emigrate to America. He worked as a gardener in the East and later farmed in Michigan, where he resolved to join the Michigan Cavalry because he abhorred slavery and felt a patriotic obligation to his new country. The Civil War had brought him to East Tennessee, where his service record and his steadying Christian influence on other soldiers had been exemplary. He was one of many Northern veterans who had returned to East Tennessee to rebuild their lives after the war. Pointedly, Hughes had Mr. Hill conclude his life story with these remarks directed to his neighbors:

. . . I came to this place on the mountains, which I knew was healthy, and would suit me. Well, they all said I should be starved out in two years and have to quit, but before three years were out I was selling them corn, and better bacon than they'd ever had before. Some of 'em begin to think I'm right now, and there's a deal of improvement going on, and if they'd only, as I tell 'em, just put in all their time on their farms, and not go loafing round gunning, contented with corndodgers and a bit of pork, and give up whisky, they might all do as well as I've done. I should like to go back once more and see the old country; but I mean to end my days here. There's no such country that I ever saw. The Lord has done all for us here. And it seems like dreams that I should live to see a Rugby up here on the mountains" (76).

As critics were quick to point out, the young British gentlemen needed Amos Hill's sermon on hard work as much as his native neighbors did. In contrast to Amos Hill, who began life as an estate laborer, nothing in their background experience and temperament equipped them to succeed as Rugby farmers.[31] Perhaps a thousand public school graduates briefly passed through Rugby; some returned to Britain, while the most enterprising left for cities or western states that offered them better economic prospects. Most of the colonists who stayed in

Rugby long enough to build homes and become part of community history came in family groups; like Amos Hill, many of the British born colonists who persevered had resided elsewhere in America before moving to Rugby.[32]

Because of his wife's ill health, Hughes never lived for an extended period at Kingston Lisle, the Rugby residence that was built for him. His brother Hastings, mother Margaret, and niece Emily moved into Uffington House in 1881, and Thomas visited for a month each year until his mother's death in 1887. The Board of Aid to Land Ownership struggled with continuing difficulties over imperfect land titles, the failure of several proposed business schemes, and the fires that twice destroyed the Tabard Inn, which was the colony's most lucrative enterprise. In 1892, major investors interested in timber and minerals reorganized as the Rugby Land Company, without Hughes's participation. He had lost so much on his Rugby investment that he and Fanny had been forced to leave London for a modest residence in Chester, where Hughes accepted employment as a county judge to earn a living.[33] He continued to defray holiday travel expenses by writing sketches that were published in the *Spectator*. When Hughes died in Brighton en route to Italy on March 22, 1896, he was mourned not only by friends, but also by readers on both sides of the Atlantic who knew the man and his ideals through *Tom Brown's School Days* and through the aspirations for social reform that he expressed in *Rugby, Tennessee.*

Rugby, Tennessee
February 2007

Notes

1. In 1895 Macmillan published *Vacation Rambles,* a collection of the letters from various locations in Europe and America that Hughes, using the pen name Vacuus Viator, had published in *The Spectator* between 1862 and 1895.

2. Hughes was countering observers' reports that the young colonists were averse to the hard work. See for example "Drawbacks in the New Rugby," *New York Times,* November 29, 1880, 8, and "The New Rugby Colony: Discouraging Features of the Enterprise," *New York Times,* June 18, 1881, 1.

3. In 1874 the Tennessee Bureau of Agriculture published Commissioner Killebrew's first report, *Resources of Tennessee,* containing information comparable to that supplied for *Rugby, Tennessee.* For additional information on Killebrew's role in promoting immigration to Tennessee and his work as commissioner of agriculture, immigration, statistics, and mines, see Samuel Smith's "Joseph Buckner Killebrew and the New South Movement in Tennessee," *East Tennessee Historical Society Publications* 37 (1965): 5–22.

4. The following biographical information is drawn primarily from Edward C. Mack and W. H. G. Armytage, *Thomas Hughes, the Life of the Author of Tom Brown's Schooldays* (London: Ernest Benn, 1952).

5. Quoted in George J. Worth, *Thomas Hughes* (Boston: Twayne, 1984), 2.

6. Hughes's contributions to Christian Socialism are discussed in *Victorian Visionaries* by Brenda Colloms (London: Constable, 1982) and *The Victorian Christian Socialists* by Edward R. Norman (New York: Cambridge University Press, 1987).

7. Worth, *Thomas Hughes,* 9.

8. Quoted in Mack and Armytage, *Thomas Hughes,* 57.

9. Mack and Armytage, *Thomas Hughes,* 57.

10. Ibid., 60.

11. Ibid., 65, 217.

12. Ibid., 78.

13. For discussion of Hughes's writings, see George J. Worth, *Thomas Hughes* (Boston: Twayne, 1984).

14. Mack and Armytage, *Thomas Hughes,* 170–71.

15. Ibid., 155–56.

16. Quoted in Mack and Armytage, *Thomas Hughes,* 222.

17. Early twentieth-century publications relied heavily on recollections that greatly obscured the role that Franklin W. Smith and his Boston associates played in establishing Rugby. The following reconstruction of events is based on primary documents in the Historic Rugby Archives and Special Collections at the University of Tennessee Library. For details see Benita J. Howell, "Rugby, Tennessee's Master Planner: Franklin Webster Smith of Boston," *Journal of East Tennessee History* 73 (2001): 23–38.

18. *Colonization of the Cumberland Plateau,* Bulletin no. 3 of the Board of Aid to Land Ownership (Boston, 1880).

19. Rugby never was abandoned. The colony manager, Robert Walton, and his son Will Walton continued to live in Rugby, protect its public buildings, and preserve the documents now held in the Tennessee State Library and Archives and Historic Rugby Archives.

20. Mark Twain and Charles Dudley Warner, *The Gilded Age: A Tale of Today* (Hartford, CT: American Publishing Co., 1873).

21. John Muir, "Crossing the Cumberland Mountains," in *A Thousand-Mile Walk to the Gulf* (Boston: Houghton Mifflin, 1916), quoted from the full-text edition posted in the Sierra Club John Muir Exhibit (*http://www.sierraclub.org/john%5Fmuir%5Fexhibit/*), accessed January 30, 2007.

22. A. R. Hogue mentioned the falls and cave attractions of Rock Castle Creek in his *History of Fentress County, Tennessee* (Nashville: Williams Printing Co., 1916), 7. Rock Castle

Creek flows southwest from Jamestown to its confluence with Buffalo Cove Creek.

23. "Victorian Environmental Planning in Rugby, Tennessee," by Benita J. Howell and Susan E. Neff, in *Culture, Environment, and Conservation in the Appalachian South* (University of Illinois Press, 2002), 170–81.

24. W. B. Hesseltine, "Tennessee's Invitation to Carpetbaggers," *East Tennessee Historical Society Publications* 4 (January 1932): 102–15.

25. Franklin Webster Smith to Oliver P. Temple, August 28, 1878, Oliver P. Temple Collection, Special Collections Department, University of Tennessee Library. See also Fred A. Bailey, "Legalities, Agriculture, and Immigration: The Role of Oliver Perry Temple in the Rugby Experiment," *East Tennessee Historical Society Publications* 44 (1972): 90–103.

26. See, for example Edward King's enthusiastic description of developments in Chattanooga and Rockwood in his 1875 work *The Great South,* edited by W. M. Drake and R. R. Jones (Baton Rouge: Louisiana State University Press, 1972), 532–35.

27. Hesseltine, "Tennessee's Invitation to Carpetbaggers," describes immigration recruitment efforts during the Brownlow administration. Commissioner of Immigration Hermann Bokum established the model for Killebrew's recruitment writings in the *Tennessee Handbook and Immigrant's Guide* (Philadelphia: J. B. Lippincott, 1868).

28. Hughes had this woman mention only troop movements, not the bushwhacking that had terrorized citizens during and after the war; surely he edited much that was unpleasant out of her remarks.

29. Hughes, *Vacation Rambles,* 188.

30. John Boyle to Oliver P. Temple, February 12, 1880, Oliver P. Temple Collection.

31. Visitors who perceived these problems reported them widely through the *New York Times* and other popular media.

See for example, "Drawbacks in the New Rugby," *New York Times,* November 29, 1880, 8, and "The New Rugby Colony: Discouraging Features of the Enterprise," *New York Times,* June 18, 1881, 1.

32. C. Calvin Dickinson, "Whose Sons Settled Rugby? A Study of the Population at Rugby, Tennessee, in the 1880s," *Tennessee Historical Quarterly* 52 (Fall 1993): 192–98.

33. Hughes lost at least £7000 (Mack and Armytage, *Thomas Hughes,* 252). Translating 1880 British pounds into the purchasing power of 2005 U.S. dollars, this would approximate a $750,000 loss, according to www.measuringworth.com/calculators/exchange/.

PREFACE.

THIS book is the best answer which the founders of Rugby, Tennessee, can at present make to the large and rapidly increasing number of questions which reach them from all parts of the United Kingdom about that settlement. These inquiries, speaking roughly, are addressed mainly to three points—(1) The class of persons for whom the place is intended; (2) What it is like; (3) Its prospects.

Part I. of the book deals with the first question; and I hope will sufficiently indicate the views of the founders. They will gladly welcome any persons who like to join them; but those whom they have specially in their minds are, young men of good education and small capital, the class which, of all others, is most overcrowded to-day in England. The experience of the past six months has proved that such an outlet—indeed that many such—are needed. It has also proved that, except in rare instances, the young men who go out are not able at once to earn their living, and that they should not be sent out under the age of eighteen at earliest. The Board strongly recommend that boys and young men should be placed, for a year at least, with one of the present settlers to learn their business, which can be done at a cost of from £60 to £70 for the year's board, lodging, and teaching.

The letters to the *Spectator*, which form Part II., written on the spot last autumn (and reprinted by kind permission of the Editors), give my own first impressions of the site and surroundings, more accurately, I believe, than anything I could now write on the subject. They are printed without alteration, in order that they may remain, and be taken as, first impressions only. At the same time I may add that on going over the proofs I see scarcely anything which I should have to modify were I to sit down now to write them over again.

Part III., and especially Colonel Killebrew's report and the glossary, will enable readers to judge of the present condition and prospects of the settlement. Colonel Killebrew is the Minister of Agriculture of the State of Tennessee, and the highest authority on all matters connected with land in those parts.

The Board is glad to take this opportunity of thanking him for his valuable paper, which, coming from an entirely independent quarter, may be safely relied on as to the quality and capabilities of the soil on the plateau, in and around Rugby. They have always warned intending settlers that they will have to work hard, and with intelligence, in order to succeed in farming on the Cumberland plateau; and have stated their own conviction that such conditions are far better than those (if indeed they exist anywhere)

where settlers have only to scratch the soil to get heavy crops for any number of consecutive years. They are aware that more rapid returns may probably be looked for in other parts of the States, both in the west and to the south of Rugby, where the Alabama Southern Railway Company, through their English management, are offering great advantages to the same class of settlers for whom Rugby is intended. But there will be need of many more Rugbys before the present demand is adequately met; and, meantime, they are glad to find their own anticipations borne out, and to be able to recommend their settlement as one well fitted in all respects as a home for young Englishmen.

Readers who desire to pursue the matter further, and to watch the growth of Rugby, Tennessee, may do so by reading the monthly paper which the settlers are publishing, under the name of the *Rugbeian*, and which may be procured in this country.

RUGBY—TENNESSEE.

PART I.—OUR WILL WIMBLES.

CHAPTER I.

THE GENTLEFOLK OF ENGLAND.

A CENTURY and a half ago, more or less, the Spectator, looking round with that keen sympathetic eye of his on English life, was much exercised in his mind by the phenomenon which confronted him in the person of that handy and genial friend of Sir Roger de Coverley, Will Wimble. Now Will, as I trust almost every reader remembers, was one of the deftest of the English race in those early Georgian days. He was not only the best man at hunting a pack of hounds, or catching a fish, in the county, but was "versed in all the handicrafts of an idle man." He wove nets, trained "setting dogs," tied mayflies "to a miracle," and furnished the whole countryside with "angle-rods of his own make." He would even now and then present a pair of garters of his own knitting to the mothers or daughters of the young squires, of whom he was the chosen companion.

Sitting in his room at night, after their first meeting, the Spectator could not help feeling a secret touch

of compassion towards this honest gentleman, and much
concern how so good an heart and such busy hands
were wholly employed in trifles; that so much humanity
should be so little beneficial to others, and so much
industry so little advantageous to himself.   Will had
been tried, it seems, by his parents at divinity, law, or
physic, who, when they found his genius did not lie
that way, had given him up at length to his own
inventions.   This kind of humour, on the part of the
aristocracy, moralised the Spectator, was filling several
parts of Europe with pride and beggary, wherever they
would rather see their children starve like gentlemen
than thrive in a trade or profession that is beneath
them.

Addison, indeed, seemed to think that in England
this silly and mischievous prejudice was dying out, and
that the rising generation of Will Wimbles were likely
to be put to some kind of trade, when they showed
themselves clearly unfit for a learned profession, without losing caste.   If it were so the change worked
very slowly, for the traces of " this kind of humour "
were quite apparent a quarter of a century ago, even if
they have wholly disappeared to-day.   Probably the
great increase of the standing army and navy, and the
conquests in India in the latter half of the last and the
first half of the present centuries, which opened careers
for so many Will Wimbles, may account for the slow
progress of a reform, which in a great nation of traders,
such as the England of that period became, might have
been expected to march quickly.   At any rate, the
" silly humour " has at last been buried.   There are
to-day few gentlefolk left in England who would not
gladly see a son of theirs turn his hand to any trade

or employment under the sun by which he can fairly hope to earn an honest livelihood.

Nevertheless, and in spite of this new attitude of the English landed gentry, there can be no sort of doubt that the Will Wimbles amongst them have largely increased, and at a rate far more than in proportion to the increase of the class itself. Go through any English county and you will scarcely find a family which does not own one or more cadets, of fair average abilities, good character (the downright scapegraces having decidedly diminished), and strong bodies, who are entirely at a loose end, not knowing what in the world to turn their hands to. At the same time, the need of finding something to which they *can* turn their hands gets more pressing. For it is clear enough that the ordinary younger son's yearly allowance of £150 or £200 out of the family estate, upon which so many of them were wont to vegetate, will no longer be forthcoming, and that such boys will have to consider themselves lucky if they get a public-school education, and at the end of it are left to fight their own battle, with the help of an occasional £50 or £100 note from home at critical times.

So far we have only been thinking of the Will Wimbles who troubled the Spectator—boys of gentle birth and bringing up, the sons of the squirearchy for the most part, with no taste or capacity for study, but full of various energies and tastes which were intended to be useful to their fellow-creatures. But in our time the problem has grown in dimensions. A large class has arisen, far exceeding that of the landed gentry in numbers, whose sons are brought up essentially in the same manner as their sons, if not with precisely the same surroundings. The sons of professional men, manufacturers, merchants, go nowadays to the same schools, and acquire the same habits and notions, as the sons of the landed gentry. It may safely be said that in our time of change, when the old order gives place to the new so noiselessly, yet so swiftly, there are few more striking, and, in one aspect, more encouraging facts than this vast increase of public schools in England during the last half-century. Fifty years ago some six or seven of these were educating little more than 2000 boys, on the old lines, which they had inherited from Tudor times. To-day, what with such new foundations as Marlborough, Haileybury, Radley, Wellington, Dulwich, Clifton; and the best of the old grammar schools which have started into new life; there are upwards of forty engaged on the same work of training what may be roughly called the young gentlefolk of this country. And, happily, the aims and methods of the education they are giving have improved as rapidly as the numbers requiring it have increased; till, in the best of our schools, where extravagance is sternly controlled, and simple habits are encouraged, little remains to be wished for. Our boys, up to the age of eighteen or nineteen, have as good a chance of getting high culture, both for mind and body, as any that can be had now, or, I believe, ever could have been had, in any part of the world.

But what then? Thousands of them leave our public schools every year, and have to turn to such methods of getting a living, and to such portions of the work of the world, as they find open to them.

Now, whether it be our British incapacity for getting

rid of old tradition and settling into new grooves, or
something deeper—some law underlying and governing
the results of training of a particular kind—the fact
remains, that the sphere of work which is really open to
the English public schoolboy is still in these islands, as
in Addison's day, practically limited to the three learned
professions, the public service, and the press. Art and
science may be thrown in, but offer at present too few
and too special careers to be taken into account in his
case. He may be quite ready, even eager, to become a
trader, but the odds are heavy against his succeeding if
he does.

Of course many instances of success in trade may be
cited, but they will be found amongst the sons of old
mercantile and manufacturing firms, who have inherited
thoroughly established businesses. There are plenty
of public school men who have risen to eminence of all
kinds, in literature, politics, science, while partners in
banks, breweries, and manufacturing establishments;
but very few who have themselves established any
such business successfully. In a word, whatever may
have been the case in other times and other countries,
at this time and in our country it is plain that the
spirit of our highest culture and the spirit of our trade
do not agree together. The ideas and habits which
those who have most profited by them bring away from
English public schools, do not fit them to become successful traders.

So, in sadly increasing numbers, our Will Wimbles
within a year or two of leaving school find themselves
stranded. The clever ones of their old school-fellows,
or those with exceptional backing from friends, or exceptional power of pushing themselves, are doing well enough.

But for them ?   They have tried door after door in vain,
and are beginning to find that, for such as they, our time
is indeed a cruel one.   For every commission, cadetship,
clerkship—for every post, in short, by which a gentleman can live, however humble the outlook of it may
be, there are an hundred candidates.   One is pained
to think of what becomes of the unsuccessful ones, and
to see and hear of one and another hanging round
homes, which at best can only afford them food and
shelter, and to very many of which even that is a hard
task; or waiting in the purlieus of our great centres of
employment, in the hope, so rarely fulfilled, that something may turn up.   Such hanging round and waiting
must take the heart and hope out of them—well if it
do no worse than that—and make them every year
less and less fit to fight the battle of life, or do a good
stroke of work for themselves, or any one else.   Yes ;
of the many sad sights in our England, there is none
sadder than this, of first-rate human material going
helplessly to waste, and in too many cases beginning
to turn sour, and taint, instead of strengthening, the
national life.

Poor Will Wimbles!   In these last few years of deep
depression one has been positively haunted by them in
ever-increasing numbers—fine strong fellows, who look
with such open truthful eyes into yours, thankful for the
slightest hint, or guidance, or sympathy ; hopeful still,
ready to do *anything*, so that they may only be independent and a burthen to nobody.   It is enough to
keep one awake o' nights thinking of them, gradually
losing heart and hope ; becoming suspicious, cynical,
envious of old comrades who are succeeding ; feeling
shame or remorse over the thought of possible careers,

which, poor fellows, were never more than nominally
open to them, and so drifting on into weary, colourless,
middle age.

Here and there, no doubt, one sees them living
heroic lives in their narrow and depressing surroundings; devoting themselves to those who need such help
as even they can give; making the dens of vice and
misery in our great towns "sing with the welcome of
their feet;" spreading the light of steadfastness and
content over some humble home. All honour to these;
but they, after all, are the rare exceptions. No section
of humanity produces any large proportion of heroes,
and why should we look for them amongst our Will
Wimbles?

No. We may reckon that for something like half
the number of those who leave our public schools, and
for whom the public service, the learned professions,
or the press, would be the natural career, those careers
are blocked and practically closed.

And so, on this side of our national life, the Spectator of 1881 has in these latter days a far sadder
outlook than he of 1720, when the Will Wimbles in
a county might be counted on the fingers; were a pleasure to everybody but themselves; or, at any rate, no
burthen to the country houses, where they found their
place at table, and their sleeping-corner in the attics.

CHAPTER II.

BUT the present distress, though most severely felt amongst what we have called, for want of a more accurate term, the gentlefolk of England, by no means ends with them. The demand alluded to above for truer and higher training, which has more than quadrupled our public schools of the old type, while it has revolutionised their methods and ennobled their aims, has been equally powerful in every part of the nation. The new life is not only felt in the head, but is tingling in the extremities of the body politic. It may be fairly said, perhaps, that it was first felt in the extremities; that the impulse came from below rather than from above.

But let the impulse have come from where it will, it is here; it has produced and is producing certain results, and has to be reckoned with at every turn. And one of those results is, that in the trading class too we have much the same state of things as amongst the gentlefolk. Trade on the old lines, engaged in as a mere wealth-producing machine, is becoming distasteful to those who live by it.

This may seem a startling assertion in the face of the open and unabashed property worship, or, to call it by its right name, mammon worship of our

time; trade being still at any rate the handiest
method of making money. Surely, one may be told,
if you won't believe your own eyes, or can't see
the things which lie under your own nose, you may,
at any rate, unless you are deaf also, hear something of what the wisest seers amongst us English
have been telling us for the last fifty years. Let us
listen for a minute to him who has so recently left us.
" The word Hell," says Mr. Carlyle, " is still frequently
in use amongst the English people, but I could not
without difficulty ascertain what they meant by it.
Hell generally signifies the infinite terror, the thing a
man is infinitely afraid of, and shudders at and shrinks
from, struggling with his whole soul to escape from.
With Christians it is the infinite terror of being found
guilty before the Just Judge. And now what is it if
you pierce through his cants, his oft-repeated hearsays
what he calls his worships; what is it that the modern
English soul does in very truth dread infinitely and
contemplate with entire despair ? What *is* his Hell;
after all these reputable oft repeated hearsays, what is
it ? With hesitation, with astonishment, I pronounce
it to be the terror of not succeeding; of not making
money, fame, or some other figure in the world; chiefly
of not making money. Is not that a somewhat singular Hell ?" " Dig down where you will, through
the Parliament floor or elsewhere, how infallibly do
you, at spade's depth below the surface, come upon this
liar's-rock substratum! Much else is ornamental; true
on barrel heads, in pulpits, hustings, parliamentary
benches, but this is for ever true and truest. 'Money
does bring money's worth; put money in your purse.'
Here, if nowhere else, is the human soul still in

thorough earnest, sincere with a prophet's sincerity, and 'the Hell of the English,' as Sauertieg said, 'is the infinite terror of not getting on, especially of not making money.' "—(*Past and Present: Gospel of Mammonism.*) Is not the same note sounding through our poetry?—" Propputty, propputty, propputty, that's wut I hear 'em saay," chuckles Tennyson's modern farmer, listening to the music of his horse's feet on the road — unworthy successor to his strong old half-heathen sire. And so one might go on, quoting from all the host of popular writers, preachers, poets, novelists, dramatists, were it worth while. And what shadow of proof is forthcoming that the nation has become less in earnest in this matter; that money is not with us a growing and not a waning power; that we English have, in Carlyle's phrase, changed our Hell in the generation since *Past and Present* appeared?

To all which one can only answer, " Well, in spite of all this, and admitting fully the strength of the evidence you can pile up as to the Mammon worship, the idolatry of mere hard cash, in our England of to-day, yet, nevertheless, we English *have* changed our Hell (to accept Carlyle's test), in this generation." The change is partly due, no doubt, to his own teaching— more to the genuine religious revival, which, in spite of ritualistic trappings and universalist outbursts, has marked our time—most of all to that new spirit, referred to above, which, drawing life and nourishment from both of these, and from many other sources, has renewed and remodelled our whole ideas and methods of training our youth in this Victorian age.

The revival was in the air—a new gospel for a new time. The yearning for it—haunting the dumb masses of an earnest and honest people—would have found expression and realisation somehow, had Carlyle, Arnold, Maurice, Newman, and the other prophetic voices been silent. But its outward expression has come, as above said, in this recasting, this renewal, of our whole ideas and methods of training our youth of both sexes. And of this new gospel and time the most obvious characteristic —rapidly getting itself acknowledged and accepted as such—is (to confine ourselves to the negative side of the problem as put by Carlyle) that the " infinite terror," or Hell of us English, at any rate of the rising generation, is no longer " not making money; " is coming again to be " the being found guilty before the Just Judge."

And now, if we look at the results of this revival on the trading class, we shall find them much the same as amongst the gentlefolk. The schools to which the latter resort have, as we have seen, quadrupled in numbers; but those which are adapting themselves specially to the needs of the former are multiplying far more rapidly. There are already upwards of two hundred remodelled grammar schools, or new foundations, such as those in Devon, Norfolk, Bedfordshire, expressly designed for the sons of farmers and tradesmen; and their number is yearly increasing, the movement being only in its infancy. Its first result has been, that the old commercial academy is doomed, and that the young farmer and tradesman is bred and fed during the most receptive years of his life—when his nature is " wax to receive and marble to retain "— on precisely the same spiritual and physical, and much the same intellectual, food as the young squire, parson, lawyer, merchant. How could it be otherwise, seeing that rising county schools and revived grammar schools are governed by men of the same kind—often by the same men—who govern our great public schools; while the head and assistant masters have been, almost without exception, trained at the old public schools; have generally been under-masters at one or another of these, and have brought with them their methods and spirit. And so the most marked characteristics of the public school spirit are asserting themselves in hundreds of new centres, and in a class which, until within the last few years, never felt their influence.

Of these characteristics perhaps the most universal, and not the least valuable, is scrupulousness—a scorn of anything like sharpness or meanness—in money matters. With this the son of the farmer and retail tradesman is filled by the time he leaves school, and so he is rapidly becoming as averse to, and as unfitted for, the practices of ordinary competitive trade as the son of squire or parson. He, too, has been taught that the failure to make money is *not* the infinite terror, the thing he should struggle with his whole soul to escape from. He is finding the atmosphere of the shop more and more distasteful — antagonistic to the influences and beliefs to which he feels that he owes all that is best in himself; on which he likes to dwell in his highest moments. And so, now that all (or nearly all) careers are open to merit, he turns his back on the counter, and becomes a competitor for employment in the public service, the professions, or literature. Failing these, he drags on at the counter, a restless, unhappy mortal, he scarcely knows why; on the eager look-out for any endurable road of deliverance from a calling to which he feels he is not called. It is scarcely possible, under such circumstances, that he should be successful.

Success involves almost necessarily a sharpness in
money matters which he has learned to scorn; taking
custom away from others, old comrades as likely as not,
whom he does not want to injure, whom he would far
sooner help. And so it is well if in the end he escape
collapse and bankruptcy. In any case he feels himself always in the wrong place; that he hasn't found
the work he was meant to find in this world.

Thus the trading class too is yearly adding more
and more Will Wimbles to an already overstocked
market. And, even if the rising generation were ready
and eager to become competitive retailers, this channel
of occupation is, during these last years, sensibly narrow-
ing under their eyes. On all sides the great pike are
rapidly devouring the small ones in the troubled waters
of competitive trade. It seems very doubtful if any
of the little fish will be able to survive, and hold their
own, in the near future. It will be all indeed that the
big ones themselves will be able to do, for dangerous if
not fatal rivals are threatening them also.

The spirit of combination, or co-operation, is in the
air, with what results, as regards our trading classes,
the scores of sales at or below cost prices, which
are constantly in progress at all the chief shops and
warehouses, and the eagerness to convert all businesses
into some form of company or association, show with
startling clearness. Are not even the older generation,
we may ask, bred and born as they were to the business, beginning to get tired, if not ashamed of the sore
scramble, trampling on one another, throttling one
another, which our trade has become? *Laissez faire,*
and the acknowledged law of self-interest—enlightened
and unenlightened—have had full swing, have gone

ahead scornfully, with their heads in the air, these
thirty years and upwards, and have landed us just
here.   Our shopkeepers can no longer thrive, even if
they can live, except by puffing and selling shoddy, and
treading one another under foot ; and the rising generation, at any rate, are sick of such ways of living ; are
resolved, so far as they are concerned, not to live in these
ways.   The nation, meantime, has also waked up to the
wastefulness and thriftlessness of the old methods of supplying its needs ; is fairly tired of puffing and shoddy ;
and in all kinds of combinations, Industrial societies,
Civil Service stores, Army and Navy stores, and the
like, is learning in a masterful manner to supply its
own wants, honestly and directly, without recourse to
puffing, shoddy, or sales at ruinous sacrifices.

That the change is an entirely wholesome one for
the nation, bringing back health and sound prosperity
to trade, no one now doubts ; but in the process,
involving, as it must, the disappearance and absorption
into the producing class of a large number of distribu-
tors or middle men, there must be much temporary
distress.   During this process of absorption we shall
have in our midst, on our hands, large numbers of
young men of the trading class, glad indeed to be once
for all emancipated from the necessity of selling shoddy
by puffing and treading one another under foot, but
with the same necessity as the Will Wimbles, of getting an honest living somehow, and the same difficulty
of ascertaining how this is to be accomplished.

And so the question recurs again — What is to
become of them ?   How is this fine human material,
this " vast overplus of might," to be set to honest work
for their own good and the good of the nation ?

CHAPTER III.

But have we even yet faced the whole of our present national distress in this department? Pressing as this question of new and wholesome outlets for our gentry and trading class has of late become, is it not a much older one, now become chronic, with the great mass of our people who live by the labour of their hands—handicraftsmen as they are named in our old tongue? And again, are not these they who need help most, and the helping of whom will bring back health most quickly to the national circulation, and enable heart and lungs and brain to play more freely?

Now it will probably in these days be generally admitted—and is certainly the opinion of this writer—that the condition of the handicraftsman is the one which most concerns this, and all other nations. And for this simple reason, that if the base of a pyramid is strong and sound, we need feel little anxiety about the upper portions. Where this is so, the worst that can happen to the upper parts is, gently to crumble away; but, even then, they will just filter down into the interstices, filling up the gaps in the structure, and wherever they stop helping to strengthen the foundations. Their disappearance may perhaps injure the picturesqueness of the building, but will not undermine its strength. The vital point is, to look to foundations.

But admitting all this to the fullest extent — admitting further, that, in spite of the great improvement in the condition and prospects of English manual labourers in the last thirty years, very much remains to be done before we can feel anything like security as to the foundations of our social pyramid—we may safely leave our handicraftsmen on one side in considering the question intended to be raised in these pages. For we are concerned here with the Will Wimbles, with those for whom there is no visible prospect of even moderately satisfactory careers in the England of to-day, and of these there are really none amongst our handicraftsmen.

A moment's consideration will make this clear enough to any one who will put the young trader and the young handicraftsman side by side, and look at them fairly. The position of the former is best put by Emerson, whose weighty words readers will thank us for using instead of our own. "The young man," he writes, "on entering life finds the way to lucrative employment blocked with abuses. The ways of trade are grown selfish to the borders of theft, and supple to the borders (if not beyond the borders) of fraud. The employments of commerce are not intrinsically unfit for a man or less genial to his faculties, but these are now in their general course so vitiated by derelictions and abuses, at which all connive, that it requires more vigour and resources than can be expected of every young man to right himself in them ; he is lost in them ; he cannot move hand or foot in them. Has he genius and virtue ? the less does he find them fit for him to grow in; and, if he would thrive in them, he must sacrifice all the brilliant dreams of boyhood and youth as dreams; he must forget the prayers of his childhood; he must take on him the harness of routine and obsequiousness. If not so minded," he adds, and we continue the quotation, though it anticipates our subject somewhat, "nothing is left him but to begin the world anew, as he does who puts a spade into the ground for food."

Emerson is of course speaking of the United States, but so stands the case with the young trader or distributor in this country also. He finds at once that the mere simple honest doing of his work will not ensure success in the grocery, hardware, haberdashery, or other business to which he has been bred. On the contrary, humiliating as it is to confess, the never-so-faithful selling of his goods for what they really are—giving full weight and measure, and keeping back no information which the buyer ought to have, as between man and man—is sure to result in no profit, and consequent bankruptcy and ruin. Faithfulness, simplicity, thoroughness, he finds only too surely will not help, but hinder him, in his day's work.

But now let us see how it stands with the young handicraftsman—the carpenter, smith, mason, ploughman, and the rest. He, happy fellow, on the other hand, has only to do his work faithfully, simply, thoroughly, to ensure success in his career. If he is able—as if faithful, simple, thorough, he assuredly soon will be—to be his own employer, so much the better for him. If not, there is scarcely an employer in England who does not desire these qualities above all others in his workmen—who is not willing and

C

eager to pay well for all the faithfulness, simplicity, thoroughness, he can get put into his work.
Like wisdom, " they cannot be gotten for gold, neither
shall silver be weighed for the price thereof;" but
even in these days they command that which cannot
command them.   Faithfulness, simplicity, thoroughness in all productive work will yet bring gold and
silver to the handicraftsman, and, what is better, a
good conscience to himself, and health to the nation
of which he is a member.   There is, alas, plenty of
scamped work in our England of to-day, in all departments of human activity ; but whatever the case may
be with others, our handicraftsmen have *no need* to
scamp their work in order to prosper, even pecuniarily.
This, let us always thankfully remember, still remains
a wholesome and encouraging fact, that faithfulness in
daily work is, as surely as ever, the road to success for our handicraftsman, who has thus his own
career more thoroughly under his own control, to
make or to mar, than any other class, and will still
find his prosperity in it duly apportioned to his own
faithfulness.

Then, as regards over-population.   It is much more
doubtful here than in the other classes whether there
is any real need for our handicraftsmen to scatter in
search of employment elsewhere.   Is there any town
or hamlet at this moment where a carpenter or smith
who will do his best cannot get employment at better
wages than his father earned ?   It is true there is no
more room for dawdlers here than elsewhere, for those
who assume that they have a right to live without
work, that somebody is bound to find them in food,
clothes, and lodging.   But how our dawdling classes

are to be dealt with is a different question, outside our present inquiry.

Whether this state of things will continue as regards our handicraftsmen depends upon themselves. If it were indeed true that English work of all kinds is deteriorating, and has already become so much less trustworthy than that of other nations, that we shall no longer buy English goods if we want the best we can get, then the look-out, not for our handicraftsmen only but for the whole nation, is as black as can be. But there is really no proof as yet of any such deterioration. If there were, English goods would not be heavily weighted by duties in all the markets of the world. There is every probability that the national position, won by so many generations of silent dogged work, will be maintained in the future—and if so it will be in a time when "labour will be king," and by no means inclined, any more than other reigning families, to put the great inheritance on one side.

It would be greatly for the advantage of our public life, and indeed for our chances of healthy progress of all kinds in the future, if statesmen and other prominent persons would realise this fact a little more clearly, that labour is going to be king. It may be a distasteful one, but is as certain as that we are in the last quarter of the century. Put as shortly as may be the case of the English handicraftsman may be stated somehow thus: Up to 1830, you, the gentlefolk, had your chance ; you wielded all the forces of this nation, and could build up the national life in whatever shape seemed best to you; and you landed England on the verge of revolution and bankruptcy. For the last half century, you, the trading or middle class, have in like

manner had your chance, and you have brought trade
to a pass that honest men can't live by it; and production to a jealous armistice, alternating with open
war, between employers and employed. Now our turn
has come; our ideas will have to prevail, and we mean
to show that they are better adapted to make a nation
what a nation should be than those of kings, or nobles,
or traders.

That the handicraftsman will use power less self-
ishly than the previous owners of it seems probable.
Not that the men themselves are individually at all
wiser or better than their predecessors, but the conditions of their advance to power have been of necessity
more purifying and ennobling.   For an aristocracy, or
great trading class, may seize and hold power by family
and individual energy, astuteness, self-assertion; but
the handicraftsmen can only do it by some form of
association.   The sticks are weak individually, but,
bound together, are stronger than any tree.   How far
in the future they may absorb the surplus of the other
classes in their ranks remains to be seen, but from all
the signs of the times it seems not improbable that the
Will Wimbles in another generation may find their best
chance of satisfactory daily bread, and general useful-
ness, in some form of manual labour at home.   At present in England the handicraftsman's career is not really
open to any one not born in the ranks.   Outsiders
would find themselves met by two obstacles, which
few could overstep if they tried, and fewer would care
to try; the jealousy and distrust of the working class,
and the prejudice of their own against what would
be considered loss of caste.   Until a young man's
mother and sister, and the girl he danced with last

night, learn to see him driving a plough, or working at a bench or forge for wages, without any sense
of humiliation, those occupations cannot fairly be said
to be open to him.   In the Colonies, and in America
(out of the Eastern cities) this is so, and it would be
well if it were so at home; for a country cannot be in
a thoroughly healthy state in which handicrafts are
looked down upon.   Such healthy signs as the establishment of workshops at all our best public schools
seem to show that the wiser time is not far off.   But
it is not yet.

And so we may dismiss the great bulk of the
nation from our thoughts for the present, and fall back
on our original problem, What outlet of a satisfactory
kind can be found for the swarming manhood of the
English gentry and middle class?

CHAPTER IV.

It follows from the above considerations, and indeed
has been only too manifest this long while past, to
many anxious persons, responsible in one way or
another for, or interested in, those whom we have
called our Will Wimbles, that these islands can no
longer sustain them with advantage to themselves or
others. There is no work for them, of a reasonably
hopeful kind, at home ; nor any prospect of such in
the immediate future. So here they cannot stay without detriment to themselves and to the nation. Our
English distemper is, in short, a determination of blood
to the head and heart ; and the remedy, to carry it to
the extremities. To this we have to make up our
minds, and the only question is, how best to do it, so
that in their strange life, and amongst their new surroundings, the odds may be in favour of our Will
Wimbles and not against them.

Happily, we English have advantages such as no
other race have ever had for dealing with this problem.
In every quarter of the globe there are vigorous communities in which a young Englishman will find his
mother tongue spoken, and the laws, customs, and
habits prevailing which he has left behind him. But,
great as this advantage is, it must be taken with a

set-off in looking at our present problem.   These communities of English-speaking people, far away from the
mother island, amongst whom he can scarcely feel
himself a stranger, have not as yet had time to feel
the effects of that new spirit which, if we are right, is
such a potent factor in the social revolution which is
going on at home, and has sent him abroad to seek his
fortune.   The vital change in the aims and methods
of education, which (again, if we are right) is weaning
the rising generation at home from old ideas and
habits, and making these distasteful, has not as yet
influenced our Colonies or the United States to at all
the same extent.   The " hell of the English," as Carlyle saw it,—the " infinite terror " of not making
money—still seems to remain the thing which is contemplated with entire despair, which men will struggle
with their whole soul to escape from, in these new
homes of our English race.   The young Englishman,
landing in America, Australia, New Zealand, the Cape,
even, it is to be feared, in the till lately uncorrupted
Figi, will find the trail of the serpent on all the lucrative professions and practices of man, and the race for
wealth in them even more keen than at home.   If he
is drawn into that race he will have, in the new home
as well as in the old, to sacrifice all the brilliant dreams
of boyhood and youth as dreams ; he must forget the
prayers of his childhood, and must take on him the
harness of routine and obsequiousness.   " If not so
minded," to repeat Mr. Emerson's pregnant words,
" nothing is left him but to begin the world anew, as
he does who puts the spade into the ground for
food."

It was many years before the modern communistic

doctrines were in the air, that the great American teacher was urging the claims of manual labour as a part of the education of every young man.   His words are well worth the attention of all anxious persons, in any degree responsible for the start in life of one of our Will Wimbles.   " Apart from the emphasis," he writes, " which the times give to the doctrine that the manual labour of society ought to be shared amongst all its members, there are reasons proper to every individual why he should not be deprived of it.   The use of manual labour is one which never grows obsolete, and which is inapplicable to no person.   A man should have a farm or a mechanical craft for his culture.   We must have a basis for our higher accomplishments, our delicate entertainments of poetry and philosophy, in the work of our hands.   We must have antagonism in the tough world for all the variety of our spiritual faculties, or they will not be born. Manual labour is the study of the external world. The advantage of riches remains with him who procured them, not with the heir.   When I go into my garden with a spade, and dig a bed, I feel such an exhilaration and health that I find I have been defrauding myself all this time in letting others do for me what I should have done with my own hands. But not only health but education is in the work." Again, " I do not wish to overstate this doctrine of labour, or insist that every man should be a farmer, any more than that every man should be a lexicographer. In general, however, one may say that the husbandman's is the oldest and most universal profession, and that when a man does not yet discover in himself any fitness for one work more than another, this may be

preferred.   But the doctrine of the farm is merely
this, that every man ought to stand in primary relations
with the work of the world; ought to do himself, and
not to suffer the accident of his having a purse in his
pocket, or his having been bred to some dishonourable
and injurious trade, to sever him from those duties;
and for this reason, that labour is God's education,
that he only is a sincere learner, he only can become
a master who learns the secrets of labour, and who, by
real cunning, extorts from nature her secrets."

To begin the world anew, and put spade into the
ground again for food, is the best advice then that we
have to offer.   This cannot be done here at home.   At
present there is no sufficient margin in agricultural
wages over the cost of subsistence; you, our Will
Wimbles, could at best only earn a bare living so;
whereas, if you are really willing to accept the conditions, you ought at least to be able, in a few years, to
make a good home of your own.   But for that, once
for all, land here is too costly a luxury; besides, as
already said, for the present caste prejudice against
manual labour is too strong.   You must begin, then,
across the seas somewhere—the sooner the better.

What you have to do is to discover some place on
the face of this broad planet where you may set to
work on the best conditions; where the old blunders
have the smallest chance of repeating themselves; and
those new ideas, that new spirit, which have done so
much to make England impossible for you in these
days, will have the best chance of free development.
You want to get your chance, in short, in a place
where what we have been calling the English public-
school spirit—the spirit of hardiness, of reticence, of

scrupulousness in all money matters, of cordial fellowship, shall be recognised and prevail ; so that, in your
new home, you may feel that you are able to live up
to your ideal, and are more or less helping, or at least
are not jostling or hindering, your nearest neighbours,
on the right and left.

It is, at any rate, with the view of meeting a special
demand of this kind, pressing more and more severely
year by year, on our gentry and trading classes, that
the founders of Rugby, Tennessee, have established that
settlement. The significance of the name, identified as
it is at home with the great educational movement, in
the train, and, as a consequence of which, the industrial
as well as the intellectual and spiritual life of England
is being revolutionised from top to bottom,—has been
at once recognised on both sides of the Atlantic.
There is, I think, every wish that the effort should
have a fair trial ; at any rate, encouragement of the
most gratifying kind has been forthcoming in abundance, during the few months that the matured scheme
has been before the public in the United States and at
home.

And here let me at once indicate the main lines which
have guided the founders of Rugby in deciding how
far we should go, and where we should stop, in aiding
our settlers. We have felt and seen, in many instances,
the danger and the cruelty of letting our Will Wimbles
wander out at hap-hazard with a few pounds and a
letter or two of introduction in their pockets. In the
great majority of cases a boy will go wrong at first
under such conditions—well, indeed, if he ever gets
thoroughly right again at all. Whereas, if you send
him to a place where he will fit in naturally and

easily, as a piece of the social machine already at work, and, where that machine is in a sound and healthy condition, the chances are all the other way. If he has any sterling stuff in him at all it is sure to come out then and there.

Such a machine it has been our aim to provide.

To give the old and central blunder as little chance of repeating itself as possible, we have organised and handed over the trade of the place to the settlers themselves. They can carry it on in such manner as they please, except that they cannot exclude any settler from membership who wishes to take his part in it, and will pay his five dollars for his share. If the old tricks and frauds of trade creep in, it will be no fault of the founders; and the fact of the existence of the central store and mart, open to all, will be a constant incentive to return, to any who may be straying into the old paths.

To strengthen the feeling of fellowship in a higher sphere, there is one church which is open to all, and which invites to a common worship, being the property of no single denomination, but of the community.

To give the young settler a fair chance of finding his legs, and trying what he is best fitted for before he takes any line for himself, we provide him barrack room at a cheap rate, and have arranged that all the work on our unsold lands—in gardening, planting, clearing, cultivating—shall be done by such settlers as care to undertake it, by piece work, paid for by us at the rate current in the neighbourhood. And lastly, whenever he is ready to buy land on his own account, he can get the fullest information as to price and quality, not only of our lands—to which we make not the slightest attempt to limit him—but of all land on sale in the district, so far as our information goes.

And there we leave him. If with these helps he cannot fall in with the life about him, keep himself well by his own work, and make himself an acceptable member of the new society, he is not the sort of person required for this experiment. To those who have gone with us so far, who think such an effort needed, and valuable, and care to see how this particular experiment seems likely to answer, the rest of these pages are dedicated.

PART II.

A NEW HOME—FIRST IMPRESSIONS.

CHAPTER I.

LIFE IN AN AMERICAN LINER.

SIR—It is many years since I addressed you last over this signature, indeed, I should doubt if five per cent of your present readers will remember having ever shared for a few minutes with me the delights of shooting the Iron gates on the Danube, lounging in a caique up and down the sparkling Bosphorus, shopping in the Stamboul bazaars, looking out from the Acropolis over the the Bay of Salamis and the Isthmus of Corinth, or any of the other "harvests" of a quiet (ought I to say "lazy" rather than "quiet"?) eye, which I was wont in those days, by your connivance, to submit to them in vacation times. Somehow to-day the old instinct has come back on me, possibly because I happen to be on an errand which should be of no small interest to us English just now; possibly because the last days of an Atlantic crossing seem to be so naturally provocative of the instinct for gossiping, that one is not satisfied with the abundant opportunities one gets on board the vessel in which one is a luxurious prisoner for ten days.

We have been going day and night since we left
Queenstown harbour at an average rate of eighteen
(land) miles an hour.   We are more than 1300
passengers (roughly, 200 saloon, and the rest steerage),
whose baggage, when added to the large cargo of dry
goods we are carrying, sinks our beautiful craft till
she draws twenty-four feet of water.   She herself is
more than 150 yards long, and weighs as she passes
Sandy Hook,——well, I am fairly unable to calculate
what she weighs, but as much, at any rate, as half-a-
dozen luggage-trains on shore.   We have had our last,
or the captain's dinner, at which fish, to all appearance
as fresh as if the sailors had just caught them over the
side, and lettuces as crisp as if the steward had a
nursery garden down below, have been served as part
of a dinner which would have done no discredit to a
first-class hotel; beginning with two sorts of soup, and
ending with two sorts of ices.   Similar dinners, with
other meals to match——four solid ones in the twenty-
four hours, besides odds and ends——have been served
day by day, without a hitch, in a cabin kept as sweet
as Atlantic air, constantly pumped into it by the
engine, can make it.   Considering all which, I sit
down before these voyages as the greatest mechanical
feat yet performed by "men my brothers, men the
workers," and can only say that if this is but " earnest
of the things that they shall do," I hope yet to live to
fly under equally commodious surroundings.

By the way, Sir, I may remark here, in connection
with our feeding, that if we might be taken as average
specimens of our race, there is no ground whatever for
anxiety as to the Anglo-Saxon digestion, of which
some disagreeable philosophers have spoken with dis-

respect and foreboding in recent years. There were, perhaps, ten persons whose native tongue was not English, and yet we carried our four solid meals a day with resolution bordering on the heroic. The racks were never on the tables, and we had only for a few hours a swell which thinned our ranks for two meals; and yet when I look round and make such inquiry as I can, I can see or hear of nothing more than a very slight trace of dyspepsia here and there. The principal change I remarked in the manners and customs on the voyage was the marked increase of play and betting on board. When I first crossed, ten years ago, there was nothing more than an occasional game at whist in the saloon or smoking-room. This voyage it was not easy to get out of the way of hard play, except on deck. The best corner of the smoking-room was occupied from breakfast till "Out lights" by steady poker parties, and other smaller and more casual groups played fitfully at the other tables. There were always whist and other games going on in the saloon, but of a soberer and (in a pecuniary sense) more innocent character. There were "pools" of a sovereign or a half-sovereign on every event of the day, "the run" being the most exciting issue. The drawer of the winning number seldom pocketed less than £40, when it was posted on the captain's chart at noon. I heard that play is rather favoured now than otherwise on all the lines, as a percentage is almost always paid to the funds of the Sailors' Orphan Asylum, for which excellent charity a collection is also legitimately made during every passage. We were good supporters, and collected nearly £70 at our entertainment, which I attribute partly to the fact that we had on board a

leading American actor, who most good-naturedly
" turned himself loose " for us, and that the plates at
the two doors were held by the daughters of an
English Earl, and a former American minister of
great eminence. The countries could not have been
more characteristically or charmingly represented, and
the charity owes them its best thanks.

There was the usual mine of information and entertainment to be struck with ease by the merest novice
in conversational shaft-sinking. Why is it that folk
are so much more ready to talk on an Atlantic steamer
than elsewhere? I myself " struck ile " in several directions, one of a sad kind,——Scotch farmers of the highest
type going out to select new homes, where there will
be no factors. The most remarkable of these appeared
to have made up his mind finally, when he had been
told that he would not be allowed a penny at the end
of his lease for an addition of three rooms he was
obliged to make to his house, as his family were growing up. Have landlords and factors gone mad, in face
of the serious times which are on them ?

There was quite an abundance of parsons, of many
denominations, and all of mark. Prayers on Sunday
were read by a New-England Episcopalian, and the
sermon preached by a Scotch Free Kirk minister. All
were men of broad views, in some cases verging on
Latitudinarianism to a point which rejoiced my heretic
soul,——*e.g.* a Protestant minister in a great American
western city, whose church had recently been rebuilt.
Looking round to find where his flock could be best
housed on Sundays, pending reconstruction, he found
the neighbouring synagogue by far the most convenient,
and proposed to go there. His people cordially agreed

and, despite the furious raging of the (so-called) religious Press, into the synagogue they went for their Sunday services, stayed there six months, and when they left were only charged for the gas by the Rabbi. An intimacy sprang up. It appeared that the Rabbi looked upon Our Lord as the first of the inspired men of his nation, greater than Moses or Samuel; and in the end the two congregations met at a service conducted partly by the Rabbi and partly by my informant!—a noteworthy sign of the times, but one at which I fear many even of your readers will shake their heads.

There were some Confederate officers, ready to talk without bitterness of the war, and I was very glad to improve the occasion, having never had the chance of a look from that side of the curtain. Anything more grim and humorous than the picture of Southern society during those awful four years I never hope to meet with. The entire want of regular medicines, especially bark, had been their greatest trouble, he thought. In his brigade their remedy for " the shakes " came to be a plaster of *raw turpentine*, just drawn from the pine woods, laid on down the back. Some one suggested that pills were very portable, and easily imported. " Pills," he said, scornfully, " pills, sir, were as scarce in our brigade as the grace of God in a grog-shop at midnight!" Nothing so vividly brought out to me the horrors of civil war as his account of the perfect knowledge each side had of the plans and doings on the other. A Northern officer, whom he had come to know since the war, was leaning against a post within three yards of Jef. Davis when he made his famous speech announcing the supersession of Joe Johnson as the General fronting Sherman. Sherman had heard it in a few hours,

D

and was acting on the news before nightfall. The most terrible example was that of the mining of the Richmond lines. The defenders knew almost to a foot where the mines were, and when they were to be fired. Breckenbridge's division, in which he fought, were drawn up in line to repel the attack, when the earthworks went up in the air, and the assailants rushed into the great gap which had been made, and which was nearly filled, before they fell back, with the bodies of Northern soldiers. For the last two years, in almost every battle he had all he could do to hold his own against the front attack, knowing and feeling all the while that the enemy was overlapping and massing on both flanks, and that he would have to retire his regiment before they could close. And yet they held together to the last !

> " I pity mothers, too, down South,
>   Although they sat amongst the scorners."

It is a curious experience, and one well worth trying, this ten days' voyage. When you go on board at Liverpool, and look round at the first dinner, there are probably not half a dozen faces you ever saw before. By the time you walk out of the ship, bag in hand, on to the New York landing-place, there are scarcely half a dozen with whom you have not a pleasant speaking acquaintance ; while with a not inconsiderable number you feel (unless you have had singularly bad luck) as if you must have known them intimately for years, without having been aware of it. As you touch land, the express-men and hotel touts rush on you, and the spell is broken. The little society resolves itself at their touch into separate atoms, which are whirled away, without time to wish one another God-speed,

into the turbulent ocean of New York life, never again
to be gathered together as a society in this world, for
worship, or food, or fun. "The present life of man, O
king!" said a Saxon Thane in Edwin's Witangemote,
when they were consulting whether Augustine and his
priests should be allowed to settle at Canterbury, "re-
minds me of one of your winter feasts, where you sit
with your Thanes and counsellors. The hearth blazes
in our midst, and a grateful heat is spread around,
while storms of rain and snow are raging without. A
little sparrow enters at one door and flies delighted
around us, till it departs through the other. Such is
the life of man, and we are as ignorant of the state
which went before as of that which will follow it.
Things being so," went on the Thane, "I feel that if
this new faith can give us more certainty it deserves
to be received,"—which last sentiment has, I allow, no
bearing on the present subject, nor, perhaps, you will
say, has the rest of it. But, somehow, the old story
came into my head so vividly, as I was leaving the
steamer, that I feel like tossing it on to your readers
to see what they can make of it; though I own, on
looking at it again, I am not myself clear as to the
interpretation, or whether I am the sparrow or the
Thane.

New York is more overwhelming than ever,—surely
the most tremendous human mill on this planet; but
I must not begin upon it at the end of a letter.

VACUUS VIATOR.

CHAPTER II.

EAST TENNESSEE, *September* 1, 1880.

HERE I am at my goal, and so full of new impressions
that I must put some of them down at once, lest they
should slip away like the new kind of recruits, and I
should not be able to lay my hand on them again
when I want them. The above address is vague, as
this range of highlands extends for some 200 miles
through this State and Kentucky; but, though fixed
as fate myself, I can for the moment put no more
definite heading to my letters. The name of the town
that is to be, and which is already laid out and in
course of building here, is a matter of profound interest to many persons, and not to be decided hastily.
The only point which seems clear is that it will be
some name round which cluster tender memories in
the old Motherland. We are some 1800 feet above
the sea, and after the great heat of New York, New-
port, and Cincinnati, the freshness and delight of this
brisk mountain air are quite past describing. For
mere physical enjoyment, I have certainly scarcely
ever felt its equal, and can imagine nothing finer.

And now for our journey down. We left Cincinnati
early in the morning by the Cincinnati Southern Rail-

way, a line built entirely by the city, and the cost of which will probably make the municipality poor for some years to come. But it seems to me a splendid and sagacious act of foresight in a great community, to have boldly taken hold of, and opened up at once, what must be one of the main, if not the main line of communication between North and South in the future. I believe the impelling motive was the tendency of the carrying trade of late years to settle along other routes, leaving the metropolis of the South-West out in the cold.

If this be so, the result justifies the prompt courage of the citizens of Cincinnati, for the tide has obviously set in again with a vengeance. The passenger-cars are filled to the utmost of their capacity; and freight, as we know here too well, is often delayed for days, in spite of all the efforts of the excellent staff of the road. Besides its through traffic, the line has opened up an entirely new country, of which these highlands seem likely to prove a profitable, as they certainly are the most interesting, portion. This section of the line has not been open for six months, and already it is waking up life all over these sparsely-settled regions. Down below, on the way to Chatanooga, I hear that the effect is the same, and that in that great mineral region blast-furnaces are already at work, and coal-mines opening all along the line. At Chatanooga there are connections with all the great Southern lines; so that we on this aerial height are in direct communication with every important seaport from Boston to New Orleans, and almost every great centre of inland population; and the settlers here, looking forward with that sturdy faith which seems to

inspire all who have breathed the air for a week or
two, are already considering upon which favoured mart
they shall pour out their abundance of fruits and
tobacco, from the trees yet to be planted and seed yet
to be sown. All which seems to prove that Cincinnati,
at any rate, has done well to adopt the motto, "d'audace,
toujours d'audace," which is, indeed, characteristic of
this country and this time.

And the big work has not only been done, but done
well and permanently. The engineering difficulties
must have been very great; the cuttings and tunnels
had to be made through hard rock, and the bridges
over streams which have cut for themselves channels
hundreds of feet deep. We crossed the Kentucky
River, on (I believe) the highest railway bridge in the
world, 283 feet above the water; and rushed from a
tunnel in the limestone rock right on to the bridge which
spans the north fork of the Cumberland river, 170
feet below. The lightness of the ironwork on which
these bridges rest startles one at first, but experience
has shown them to be safe, and the tests to which
they have been put on this line would have tried most
seriously the strength of far more massive structures.
But it is only in its bridges that the Cincinnati Southern Railway has a light appearance. The building of
the line has a solid and permanent look, justifying,
I should think, the very considerable sum per mile
which has been spent on it above the ordinary cost in
this country. And by the only test which an amateur
is as well able to apply as an expert, that of writing
on a journey, I can testify that it is as smoothly laid
as the average of our leading English lines.

For the last fifty miles we ran almost entirely

through forests, which are, however, falling rapidly all along the side of the line, and yielding place to corn-fields in the rich bottoms, wherever any reasonably level ground bordered the water-courses, up which we could glance as we hurried past.   I was surprised, and, I need not say, greatly pleased, to see the appar-ently excellent terms on which the white and coloured people were consorting, even in the Kuklux regions through which we came.   A Northern express-man, our companion at this point, denounced it as the most lawless in the United States.   Some hundred homi-cides, he declared, had taken place in the last year, and no conviction had been obtained, the juries look-ing on such things as regrettable accidents.

This may be so, but I can, at any rate, testify, from careful observation of the mixed gangs of workmen on the road, and the groups gathered at the numerous stations, to the familiar and apparently friendly foot-ing on which the races met.   As for the decrease of the blacks, it must be in other regions than those traversed by the Cincinnati Southern Railway, for the cabins we passed in the clearings and round the stations swarmed with small urchins, clad in single garments, the most comic little figures of fun, generally, that one had ever seen, as they stood staring and signalling to the train.   There is something to me so provocative of mirth in the race, and I have found them generally such kindly folk, that I regret their absence from this same Alpine settlement,—a regret not shared, doubtless, by the few householders, to whom their constant small peculations must be very trying.

About five we stopped at the station from which this place is reached, and, turning out on the platform,

were greeted by four or five young Englishmen, who
had preceded us on one errand or another, every one
of whom was well known to me in ordinary life, but
whom for the first moment I did not recognise. I
had seen them last clothed in frock-coat and stove-
pipe hat of our much-vaunted civilisation, and behold,
here was a group which I can compare to nothing
likely to be familiar to your readers, unless it be the
company of the *Danites*, as they have been playing in
London. Broad-brimmed straw or felt hats, the latter
very battered and worse for wear; dark blue jerseys,
or flannel shirts of varying hue; breeches and gaiters,
or long boots, were the prevailing, I think I may say the
universal costume, varied according to the taste of the
wearer with bits of bright colour, laid on in handker-
chief at neck or waist. And tastes varied deliciously,
two of the party showing really a fine feeling for the
part; and one, our geologist, six feet two inches in his
stockings, and a mighty Etonian and Cantab, in brains
as well as bulk, turning out, with an heroic scorn of
all adornment, in weather-stained breeches and gaiters,
and a battered straw hat which a tramp would have
looked at several times before picking it out of the
gutter. There was a light buggy for passengers and a
mule wagon for luggage by the platform; but how
were nine men, not to mention the manager and driver,
both standing over six feet, and the latter as big at
least as our geologist, to get through the intervening
miles of forest tracks in time for tea up here? Fancy
our delight when a chorus of "Will you ride or drive?"
arose, and out of the neighbouring bushes the Danites
led forth nine saddle-horses, bearing the comfortable
half-Mexican saddles, with wooden stirrups, in use

here.   Our choice was quickly made; and, throwing
coats and waistcoats into the wagon, which the manager good-naturedly got into himself, surrendering his
horse for the time, we joined the cavalcade in our
shirts.

A lighter-hearted party has seldom scrambled
through the Tennessee mountain roads on to this
plateau.   We were led by a second Etonian, also six feet
and upwards in his stockings, whose Panama straw hat
and white corduroys gleamed like a beacon through the
deep shadows cast by the tall pine trees and white oaks.
The geologist brought up the rear, and between rode the
rest of us—all public schoolmen, I think, another
Etonian, two from Rugby, one Harrow, one Wellington
—through deep gullies, through four streams, in one of
which I nearly came to grief from not following my
leader (but my gallant little nag picked himself up like a
goat from his floundering amongst the boulders); and so
up through more open ground till we reached this city
of the future, and in the dusk saw the bright gleam
of light under the verandahs of two sightly wooden
houses.   In one of these, the temporary restaurant, we
were seated in a few minutes at an excellent tea
(cold beef and mutton, tomatoes, rice, cold apple tart,
maple syrup, etc.); and during the meal the news
passed round that the hotel, being as yet unfurnished,
and every other place filled with workpeople, we
must all (except the geologist and the Wellingtonian,
who had a room over the office) pack away in the
next frame house, which had been with difficulty
reserved for us.   If it had been a question of men
only, no one would have given it a thought; but our
party had now been swollen by two young ladies, who

had hurried down before us to visit their brother, a
settler on the plateau, and by another young Englishman, who had accompanied them.

A puzzle, you will allow, when you hear a description of our tenement. It is a four-roomed timber
house, of moderate size, three rooms on the ground
floor, and one long loft upstairs. You enter through
the verandah on a common room, 20 feet long by
14 feet broad, opening out of which are two chambers,
14 feet by 10 feet. One of these was, of course, at
once appropriated to the ladies. The second, in spite
of my remonstrances, was devoted to me, as the
Nestor of the party; and on entering it I found an
excellent bed (which had been made by two of the
Etonians), and a great basin full of wild-flowers on
the table. There were four small beds in the loft, for
which the seven drew lots; two of the losers spread
rugs on the floor of the common room, and the third
swung a hammock in the verandah.

Up drove the mule wagon with luggage, and the
way in which big and little boxes were dealt with and
distributed filled me with respect and admiration for the
rising generation. The house is ringing behind me
with silvery and bass laughter, and jokes as to the
shortness of accommodation in the matter of washing
appliances, while I sit here writing in the verandah,
the light from my lamp throwing out into strong relief
the stems of the nearest trees. Above, the vault is
blue beyond all description, and studded with stars as
bright as though they were all Venuses. The katydids
are making delightful music in the trees, and the
summer lightning is playing over the Western heaven;
while a gentle breeze, cool and refreshing as if it

came straight off a Western sea, is just lifting, every now and then, the corner of my paper.

Were I young again,—but as I am not likely to be that, I refrain from bootless castle-building, and shall turn in, leaving windows wide open for the katydid's chirp and the divine breeze to enter freely, and wishing sleep as sound as they have all so well earned, to my crowded neighbours in this enchanted solitude.

VACUUS VIATOR.

CHAPTER III.

RUGBY, TENNESSEE.

I WAS roused at five or thereabouts on the morning
after our arrival here by a visit from a big dog belonging to a native, not quite a mastiff, but more like that
than anything else, who, seeing my window wide open,
jumped in from the verandah, and came to the bed to
give me good-morning with tail and muzzle. I was
glad to see him, having made friends the previous
evening, when the decision of his dealings with the
stray hogs who came to call on us from the neighbouring forest had won my heart; but as his size and atten-
tions somewhat impeded my necessarily scanty ablutions,
I had to motion him apologetically to the window,
when I turned out. He obeyed at once, jumped out,
laid his muzzle on the sill, and solemnly, and, I
thought, somewhat pityingly, watched my proceedings.
Meantime, I heard sounds which announced the up-
rising of " the boys," and in a few minutes several
appeared in flannel shirts and trousers, bound for one
of the two rivers which run close by, in gullies 200 feet,
below us. They had heard of a pool 10 feet deep, and
found it, too; and a most delicious place it is, sur-
rounded by great rocks, lying in a copse of rhododendrons, azaleas, and magnolias, which literally form

the underwood of the pines and white oak along these
gullies.   The water is of a temperature which allows
folk whose blood is not so hot as it used to be to lie
for half an hour on its surface, and play about without
a sensation of chilliness.   On this occasion, however, I
preferred to let them do the exploring, and so at 6.15
went off to breakfast.

This is the regular hour for that meal here, dinner
at twelve, and tea at six.   There is really no difference
between them, except that we get porridge at breakfast
and a great abundance of vegetables at dinner.   At all
of them we have tea and fresh water for drink, plates
of beef or mutton, apple sauce, rice, tomatoes, peach
pies or puddings, and several kinds of bread.   As the
English garden furnishes unlimited water and other
melons, and as the settlers — young Englishmen, who
come in to see us—bring sacks of apples and peaches
with them, and as, moreover, the most solvent of the
boys invested at Cincinnati in a great square box full
of tinned viands of all kinds, you may see at once that
in this matter of provender we are not genuine objects
either for admiration or pity.

I must confess here to a slight disappointment.
Having arrived at an age myself when diet has become
a matter of indifference, I was rather chuckling as
we came along over the coming short-commons up
here, when we got fairly loose in the woods, and the
excellent discipline it would be for the boys, especially
the Londoners, to discover that the human animal can
be kept in rude health on a few daily crackers and
apples, or a slap-jack and tough pork.   And now,
behold, we are actually still living amongst the flesh-
pots, which I had fondly believed we had left in your

Eastern Egypt; and I am bound to add, "the boys"
seem as provokingly indifferent to them as if their
beards were getting grizzled. One lives and learns;
but I question whether these States are quite the place
to bring home to our Anglo-Saxon race the fact that
we are an over-fed branch of the universal brotherhood.
Tanner, I fear, has fasted in vain.

Breakfast was scarcely over when there was a
muster of cavalry. Every horse that could be spared
or requisitioned was in demand for an exploring ride to
the west, and soon every charger was bestrid by "a boy"
in free-and-easy garments, and carrying a blanket for
camping out. Away they went under the pines and
oaks, a merry lot, headed by our geologist, who knows
the forest by this time like a native, and whose shock-
ing old straw blazed ahead in the morning sun like,
shall we say, "the helmet of Navarre," or Essex's white
hat and plumes before the Train Bands, as they crowned
the ridge where Falkland fell, and his monument now
stands, at the battle of Newbury. Charles Kingsley's
lines came into my head, as I turned pensively to my
table in the verandah to write to you :—

" When all the world is young, lad, and all the trees are green,
    And every goose a swan, lad, and every lass a queen,—
Then heigh for boot and horse, lad, and round the world away,
    Young blood must have its course, lad, and every dog his day!"

Our two lasses are, undoubtedly, queens out here. The
thought occurs, are our swans—our visions, already so
bright, of splendid crops, and simple life, to be raised
and lived in this fairyland—to prove geese ? I hope
not. It would be the downfall of the last castle in
Spain I am ever likely to build.

On reaching our abode I was aware of the forester

coming across from the English garden, of which he has
charge, followed by a young native.	He walked up to
me, and announced that they were come across to tidy
up, and *black the boots*.	Here was another shock, that
we should be followed by the lumber of civilisation so
closely!	Will boots be blacked, I wonder, in the New
Jerusalem?	I was at first inclined to protest, while
they made a collection, and set them out on the verandah, but the sight of the ladies' neat little high-lows
made me pause.	These, at any rate, it seemed to me,
should be blacked, even in the Millennium.	Next minute
I was so tickled by a little interlude between the forester
and the native, that all idea of remonstrance vanished.
The latter, contemplating the boots and blacking-pot
and brushes—from under the shapeless piece of old
felt which he wore by way of hat, of the same mys-
terious colour as the ragged shirt and breeches, his only
other garments—joined his hands behind his back, and
said, in their slow way, " Look 'ere, Mr. Hill, ain't this
'ere pay-day?"	The drift was perfectly obvious.	This
citizen had no mind to turn shoeblack, and felt like
discharging himself summarily.	Mr. Hill, who was
already busily sweeping the verandah, put down his
broom, and after a short colloquy, which I did not
quite catch, seized on a boot and brush, and began
shining away with an artistic stroke worthy of one of
the Shoeblack Brigade at the London Bridge Station.
The native looked on for a minute, and then slowly
unclasped his hands.	Presently he picked up a boot,
and looked round it dubiously.	I now took a hand
myself.	If there was one art which I learned to per-
fection at school, and still pride myself on, it is shining
a boot.	In a minute or two my boot was beginning

"to soar and sing," while the forester's was already a
thing of beauty. The native, with a grunt, took up
the spare brush, and began slowly rubbing. The victory
was complete. He comes now and spends two hours
every morning over his new accomplishment, evidently
delighted with the opportunity it gives him for loafing
and watching the habits of the strange occupants, for
whom also he fetches many tin pails of water from the
well, in a slow, vague manner. He has even volun-
teered to "fix up" the ladies' room and fill their bath
(an offer which has been declined with thanks), but I
doubt whether he will ever touch the point of a genuine
" shine."

They are a curious people, these natives, the forester
(an Englishman some thirty years in this country),
told me, as we walked off to examine the English
garden, but I must keep his experiences and my own
observation for separate treatment. The English garden is the most advanced, and, I think, the most important and interesting feature of this settlement. If
young Englishmen of small means are to try their
fortunes here, it is well that they should have trustworthy guidance at once as to what are the best crops
to raise. With this view Mr. Hill was placed, in the
spring of this year, in charge of the only cleared
space available. All the rest is beautiful open forest-
land. You can ride or drive almost anywhere under
the trees, but there is no cultivated spot for many
miles, except small patches here and there of carelessly
sown maize and millet, and a rood or two of sweet
potatoes.

The forester had a hard struggle to do anything
with the garden at all this season. He was only put

in command in May, six weeks at least too late. He could only obtain the occasional use of a team, and his duties in the forest, and in grading and superintending the walks, interfered with the garden. Manure was out of the question, except a little ashes, which he painfully gathered here and there from the reckless log-fires which abound in the woods. He calls his garden a failure for the year. But as half-an-acre, which was wild forest-land in May, is covered with water-melons and cantalupes, as the tomatoes hang in huge bunches, rotting on the vines for want of mouths enough to eat them, as the Lima beans are yielding at the rate of two hundred and fifty bushels an acre, and as cabbages, sweet potatoes, beets, and squash, are in equally prodigal abundance, the prospect of making a good living is beyond all question, for any one who will set to work with a will.

In the afternoon I inspected the hotel, nearly completed, on a knoll in the forest, between the English garden and this frame house. It is a sightly building, with deep verandahs prettily latticed, from which one gets glimpses through the trees of magnificent ranges of blue forest-covered mountains. We have named it the Tabard, at the suggestion of one of our American members, who, being in England when the old Southwark hostelry from which the Canterbury Pilgrims started was broken up and the materials sold by auction (to make room for a hop store), bought some of the old banisters, which he has reverently kept till now. They will be put up in the hall of the new Tabard, and marked with a brass-plate and inscription, telling, I trust to many generations, of the place from which they came. The Tabard, when finished, as it will be

E

in a few days, will lodge some fifty guests; and, in spite of the absence of alcoholic drinks, has every chance, if present indications can be trusted, of harbouring and sending out as cheery pilgrims as followed the Miller and the Host, and told their world-famous stories as they rode through Kent five hundred years ago.

The drink question has reared its baleful head here, as it seems to do all over the world. The various works had gone on in peace till the last ten days, when two young natives "toted over" some barrels of whisky, and broached them in a shanty, on a small lot of no-man's land in the woods, some two miles from hence. Since then there has been no peace for the manager. First, one or two labourers were suddenly missing from the work on the road; then a mechanic became incompetent here and there, on the hotel, or at the saw-mills; till on Saturday last the crisis came, and some twenty men got drunk and gambled all through Sunday, getting very near a free fight in the end; and on Monday half the work collapsed. Happily the feeling of the community is vigorously temperate, so energetic measures are on foot to root out the pest. A wise State law enacts that no liquor store shall be permitted, under heavy penalties, within four miles of an incorporated school; so we are pushing on our school-house and organising a board to govern it. Meantime, we have evidence of unlawful sale (in quantities less than a pint) and of encouraging gambling, by these pests, and hope to make an example of them at the next sitting of the County Court. This incident has decided the question for us. If we are to have influence with the poor whites and blacks, we must be

above suspicion ourselves.   So no liquor will be pro-
curable at the Tabard, and those who need it will have
to import for themselves.

A bridle-path leads from the hotel down to the
Clear Fork, one of the streams at the junction of which
the town site is situate.   The descent is about 200 feet,
and the stream, when you get to it, from 30 feet to 50
feet wide,—a mountain stream, with deep pools and big
boulders.   Your columns are not the place for descriptions of scenery, so I will only say that these gorges
of the Clear Fork and White Oak are as fine as any of
their size that I know in Scotland, and not unlike in
character, with this difference, that the chief underwood consists of rhododendron (called laurel here),
azalea, and a kind of magnolia I have not seen before,
and of which I cannot get the name.   I passed huge
faggots of rhododendron, 12 feet and 14 feet long, lying
by the walks which had been cleared away ruthlessly
while grading them.   They are three miles long, and
cost under £100, a judicious outlay, I think, even
before an acre of land has been sold.   They have been
named the Lovers' Walks, appropriately enough, for no
more well-adapted place could possibly be found for
that time-honoured business, especially in spring, when
the whole gorges under the tall pines and white oak
are one blaze of purple, yellow, and white blossom.

On my return to the plateau, my first day's experiences came to an end in a way which no longer surprised me, after the boot-blacking and the Lovers'
Walks.   I was hailed by one of "the boys," who had
been unable to obtain a mount, or had some business
which kept him from exploring.   He was in flannels,
with racquet in hand, on his way to the lawn-tennis

ground, to which he offered to pilot me. In a minute
or two we came upon an open space, marked, I see on
the plans, "Cricket Ground," in which rose a fine
strong paling, enclosing a square of 150 feet, the up-
rights being six feet high, and close enough to keep
not only hogs out but tennis-balls in. Turf there was
none, in our sense, within the enclosure, and what
there must have once been as a substitute for turf had
been carefully cleared off on space sufficient for one
full-sized court, which was well marked out on the
hard sandy loam. A better ground I have rarely seen,
except for the young sprouts of oak and other scrub,
which here and there were struggling up, in a last
effort to assert their "ancient, solitary reign." At
any rate then and there, upon that court, I saw two
sets played in a style which would have done credit
to a county match (the young lady, by the way, who
played far from the worst game of the four, is the
champion of her own county). This was the opening
match, the racquets having only just arrived from
England, though the court has been the object of tender solicitude for six weeks or more to the four Englishmen already resident here, or near by. The Rugby
Tennis Club consists to-day of seven members, five
English and two native, and will probably reach two
figures within a few days, on the return of the. boys.
Meantime the effect of their first practice has been that
they have resolved on putting a challenge in the Cincinnati and Chatanooga papers offering to play a match
—best out of five sets—with any club in the United
States. Such are infant communities in these lati-
tudes !

You may have been startled by the address at the

head of this letter.   It was adopted unanimously on our return in twilight from the tennis-ground, and application at once made to the State authorities for registration of the name, and establishment of a post-office.   It was sharp practice thus to steal a march on the three Etonians, still far away in the forest.   Had they been present, possibly Thames might have pre-vailed over Avon.　　　　　　　　VACUUS VIATOR.

CHAPTER IV

A FOREST RIDE.

THERE are few more interesting experiences than a ride
through these southern forests. The scrub is so low
and thin, that you can almost always see away for long
distances amongst pine, white oak, and chestnut trees;
and every now and then at ridges where the timber is
thin, or where a clump of trees has been ruthlessly
"girdled," and the bare, gaunt skeletons only remain
standing, you may catch glimpses of mountain ranges
of different shades of blue and green, stretching far
away to the horizon. You can't live many days up
here without getting to love the trees even more, I
think, than we do in well-kempt England; and this
outrage of "girdling," as they call it—stripping the
bark from the lower part of the trunk, so that the
trees wither and die as they stand—strikes one as a
kind of household cruelty, as if a man should cut off
or disfigure all his wife's hair. If he wants a tree for
lumber or firewood, very good. He should have it.
But he should cut it down like a man, and take it
clean away for some reasonable use, not leave it as a
scarecrow to bear witness of his recklessness and lazi-
ness. Happily not much mischief of this kind has
been done yet in the neighbourhood of Rugby, and a

stop will now be put to the wretched practice.   There
is another, too, almost as ghastly, but which, no doubt,
has more to be said for it.   At least half of the largest
pines, alongside of the sandy tracts which do duty for
roads, have a long, gaping wound in their sides, about
a yard from the ground.   This was the native way of
collecting turpentine, which oozed down and accumulated at the bottom of the gash; but I rejoice to say
it no longer pays, and the custom is in disuse.   It
must be suppressed altogether, but carefully and gently.
It seems that if not persisted in too long, the poor,
dear, long-suffering trees will close up their wounds,
and not be much the worse; so I trust that many of
the scored pines, springing forty or fifty feet into the
air before throwing out a branch, which I passed in
sorrow and anger on my first long ride, may yet out-
live those who outraged them.   Having got rid of my
spleen, excited by these two diabolic customs, I can
return to our ride, which had otherwise nothing but
delight in it.

The manager, an invaluable guest from New York,
a doctor who had served on the Sanitary Commission
through the war, and I, formed the party.   The manager drove the light buggy, which held one of us also,
and the hand-bags; while the other rode by the side,
where the road allowed, or before or behind, as the
fancy seized him.   We were bound for a solitary guest-
house in the forest, some seventeen miles away, in the
neighbourhood of a cave and waterfall, which even here
have a reputation, and are sometimes visited.   We
allowed three and a half hours for the journey, and it
took all the time.   About five miles an hour on wheels
is all you can reckon on, for the country roads, sandy

tracks about 10 feet broad, are just left to take care of themselves, and wherever there is a sufficient declivity to give the rain a chance of washing all the surface off them, are only a heap of boulders of different sizes. But, after all, five miles an hour is as fast as you care to go, for the play of the sunlight amongst the varied foliage, and the new flora and fauna, keep you constantly interested and amused. I never regretted so much my ignorance of botany, for I counted some fourteen sorts of flowers in bloom, of which golden-rod and Michaelmas daisy were the only ones I was quite sure I knew—and, by the way, the daisy of Parnassus, of which I found a single flower growing by a spring. The rest were like home flowers, but yet not identical with them, at least I think not ; and the doubt whether one had ever seen them before or not was provoking. The birds — few in number — were all strangers to me ; buzzards, of which we saw five at one time, quite within shot, and several kinds of hawk and woodpecker, were the most common ; but at one point, quite a number of what looked like very big swifts, but without the dash in their flight of our bird, and with wings more like curlews', were skimming over the tree tops. I only heard one note, and that rather sweet, a cat-bird's the doctor thought ; but he was almost as much a stranger in these woods as I. Happily, however, he was an old acquaintance of that delightful insect the " tumble-bug," to which he introduced me on a sandy bit of road. My new acquaintance took no notice of me, but went on rolling his lump of accumulated dirt three times his own size backwards with his hind legs, as if his life depended on it. Presently his lump came right up against a

stone, and stopped dead. It was a "caution" to see
that bug strain to push it further, but it wouldn't
budge all he could do. Then he stopped for a moment
or two, and evidently made up his small mind that
something must be wrong behind, for no bug, he well
knew, could have pushed harder than he. So he
quitted hold with his hind legs, and turned round to
take a good look at the situation, in order, I suppose,
to see what must be done next. At any rate he presently caught hold again on a different side, and so
steered successfully past the obstacle. There were a
number of them working about, some single and some
in pairs, and so full of humour are their doings that I
should have liked to watch for hours.

We got to our journey's end about dusk, a five-
roomed, single-storied, wooden house, built on supports, so as to keep it off the ground. We went up
four steps to the verandah, where we sat while our
hostess, a small thin New Englander, probably seventy
or upwards, but as brisk as a bee, bustled about to get
supper. The table was laid in the middle room, which
opened on the kitchen at the back, where we could see
the stove, and hear our hostess's discourse. She boiled
us two of her fine white chickens admirably, and served
with hot bread, tomatoes, sweet potatoes, and several
preserves, of which I can speak with special praise of
the huckleberry, which grows, she said, in great
abundance all round. *The boys*, we heard, had been
there to breakfast after sleeping out, and not having
had a square meal since they started from Rugby.
Luckily for us her chickens are a very numerous as well
as beautiful family, or we should have fared badly.

She and her husband supped after us, and then

came and sat with us in the balcony, and talked away
on all manner of topics, as if the chances of discourse
were few, and to be made the most of.   They had lived
during the war at Jamestown close by, a village of some
eight or ten houses, and had seen the Federal and Confederate cavalry pass through again and again.   They
had never molested her or hers in any way, but had a
fancy for poultry, which might have proved fatal to
her white family but for her Yankee wit.   She and
her husband managed to fix up a false floor in one of
their rooms in which they fed the roosters ; so whenever
a picket came in sight her call would bring the whole
family out of the woods and clearing into the refuge,
where they remained peacefully amongst corn-cobs till
the danger had passed.   She had nothing but good to
say of her native neighbours, except that they could
make nothing of the country.   " The Lord had done all
he could for it," she summed up, and " Boston must take
hold of the balance."   We heard the owls all night, as
well as the katydids, but they only seemed to empha-
sise the forest stillness.   The old lady's beds, to which
we retired at ten, after our long gossip in the balcony,
were sweet and clean, and I escaped perfectly scathe-
less, a rare experience, I was assured, in these forest
shanties.   I was bound however to admit, in answer
to our hostess's searching inquiries, that I had seen,
and slain, though not felt, an insect suspiciously like
a British B flat.

The cave which we sought out after breakfast was
well worth any trouble to find.   We had to leave the
buggy and horses hitched up and scramble down a
glen, where presently, through a tangle of great rhododendron bushes, we came out in front of a huge rock,

with the little iron-stained stream just below us, and beyond, at the top of a sandy slope of perhaps 15 or 20 feet, the cave, like a long black eye under a red eyebrow, glaring at us. I could detect no fissure in the sandstone rock (the eyebrow), which hung over it for its whole length. The cave is said to run back more than 300 feet, but we did not test it. There would be good sitting room for 300 or 400 people along the front, and it is so obviously fitted for a conventicle that I could not help peopling it with fugitive slaves, and fancying a black Moses preaching to them of their coming exodus, with the rhododendrons in bloom all round. Maidenhair grows in tufts about the damp floor, and a creeping fern, with a bright red berry, the name of which the doctor told me, but I have forgotten, on the damp red walls. What the nook must be when the rhododendrons are all ablaze with blossom I hope some day to see.

We had heard of a fine spring somewhere in this part of the forest, and, in aid of our search for it, presently took up a boy whom we found loafing round a small clearing. He was bareheaded and barefooted, and wore an old, brown, ragged shirt turned up to the elbows, and old, brown, ragged trousers turned up to the knees. I was riding, and in answer to my invitation he stepped on a stump and vaulted up behind me. He never touched me, as most boys would have done, but sat up behind with perfect ease and balance as we rode along—a young centaur. We soon got intimate, and I found he had never been out of the forest, was fourteen, and still at (occasional) school. He could read a little, but couldn't write.

I told him to tell his master, from me, that he ought

to be ashamed of himself, which he promised to do with great glee; also, but not so readily, to consider a proposal I made him, that if he would write to the manager within six months to ask for it, he should be paid one dollar. I found that he knew nothing of the flowers or butterflies, of which some dozen different kinds crossed our path. He just reckoned they were all butterflies, as indeed they were. He knew, however, a good deal about the trees and shrubs, and more about the forest beasts. Had seen several deer only yesterday, and an old opossum with nine young, a number which took the doctor's breath away. There were lots of foxes in the woods, but he did not see them so often. His face lighted up when he was promised two dollars for the first opossum he would tame, and bring across to Rugby. After guiding us to the spring, and hunting out an old wooden cup amongst the bushes, he went off cheerily with two quarter-dollar bits in his pocket, an interesting young wild man. Will he ever bring the opossum? I doubt: but shall be sorry not to see his open wondering face again.

We got back without further incident (except flushing quite a number of quail, which must be lovely shooting in these woods), and found the boys at home, and hard at lawn-tennis and well-digging. The hogs are becoming an object of their decided animosity; and having heard of a Yankee notion——a sort of tweezers, which ring a hog by one motion, in a second——they are going to get it, and then to catch and ring every grunter who shows his nose near the asylum. Out of this there should come some fun shortly.

VACUUS VIATOR.

CHAPTER V.

RUGBY, TENNESSEE.

WHEN all is said and sung, there is nothing so interesting as the men and women who dwell on any corner of the earth; so, before giving you any further details of our surroundings, or doings, or prospects, let me introduce you to our neighbours, so far as I have as yet the pleasure of their acquaintance. And I am glad at once to acknowledge that it *is* a pleasure, notwithstanding all the talk we have heard of " mean whites," " poor white trash," and the like, in novels, travels, and newspapers. It may possibly be that we have been fortunate, and that our neighbours here are no fair specimens of the " poor whites " of the South. This, and the next three counties, are in the north-western corner of Tennessee, bordering on Kentucky. They are entirely mountain land. There are very few negroes in them, and they were strongly Unionist during the war. At present they are Republican, almost to a man. There is not one Democratic official in this county, and, I am told, that only three votes were cast for the Democratic candidates at the last State elections. They are overwhelmed by the vote of western and central Tennessee, which carries the State with the solid South; but here Union men can speak their minds freely, and cover their walls with pictures in coloured broad-sheet of the heroes of the war,—Lincoln, Governor Brownlow, Grant and his captains.   They are poor almost to a man, and live in log-huts and cabins which, at home, could scarcely be rivalled out of Ireland.   Within ten miles of this place there are possibly half-a-dozen (I have seen two) which are equal in accommodation and comfort to those of good farmers in England.   The best of these belongs to our nearest neighbour, with whom a party of us dined, at noon, the orthodox hour in the mountains, some weeks since.   He is a wiry man, of middle height, probably fifty-five years of age, upright, with finely cut features, and an eye that looks you right in the face.   He has been on his farm twenty years, and has cleared some fifty acres, which grow corn, millet, and vegetables, and he has a fine apple orchard.   We should call his farming very slovenly, but it produces abundance for his needs.   He sat at the head of his table like an old nobleman, very quiet and courteous, but quite ready to speak on any subject, and especially of the five years of the war through which he carried his life in his hand, but never flinched for an hour from his faith.   His wife, a slight, elderly person, whose regular features showed that she must have been very good-looking, did not sit down with us, but stood at the bottom of the table, dispensing her good things.   Our drink was tea and cold spring water; our viands, chickens, ducks, a stew, ham, with a profusion of vegetables, apple and huckleberry tarts, and several preserves, one of which (some kind of cherry, very common here) was of a lovely gold colour, and of a flavour which would make the fortune of a

London pastry-cook. A profusion of water-melons and
apples finished our repast; and no one need ask a
better; but I am bound to add that our hostess has
the name for giving the best square meal to be had
in the four counties.   It would be as fair to take
this as an average specimen of farmers' fare here,
as that of a nobleman with a French cook of fare of
the gentry at home.   Our host is a keen sportsman,
and showed us his flint-lock rifle, six feet long, and
weighing 18 lbs.!   He carries a forked stick as a rest,
and, we were assured, gets on his game about as
quickly as if it were a handy Westley-Richards, and
seldom misses a running deer.   The vast majority of
these mountaineers are in very different circumstances.
Most, but not all of them, own a log cabin and minute
patch of corn round it, probably also a few pigs and
chickens, but seem to have no desire to make any
effort at further clearing, and quite content to live
from hand to mouth.   They cannot do that without
hiring themselves out when they get a chance, but
are most uncertain and exasperating labourers. In the
first place, though able to stand great fatigue in hunting, and perfectly indifferent to weather, they are not
physically so strong as average English or Northern
men.   Then they are never to be relied on for a job.
As soon as one of them has earned three or four
dollars, he will probably want a hunt, and go off for it
then and there, spend a dollar on powder and shot,
and these on squirrels and opossums, whose skins may
possibly bring him in ten cents, as his week's earnings.
It is useless to remonstrate, unless you have an agreement in writing.   An Englishman, who came here
lately to found some manufactures, left in sheer

despair and disgust, saying he had found at last a place where no one seemed to care for money.   I do not say that this is true, but they certainly seem to prefer loafing and hunting to dollars, and are often too lazy, or unable, to count, holding out their small change and telling you to take what you want.   Temperate as a rule, they are sadly weak when wild-cat whisky —or " moonshine," as the favourite illicit beverage of the mountains is called—crosses their path.   This is the great trouble on pay nights at all the works which are starting in this district.   The inevitable booth soon appears, with the usual accompaniment of cards and dice, and probably a third of your men are thenceforth without a dime, and utterly unfit for work on Mondays, if you are lucky enough to escape dangerous rows amongst the drinkers.   The State laws give summary methods of suppressing the nuisance, but they are hard to work, and though public sentiment is vehemently hostile to whisky, the temptation proves in nine cases out of ten too strong.   The mountaineers are in the main well-grown men, though slight, shockingly badly clothed, and sallow from chewing tobacco ; suspicious in all dealings at first, but hospitable, making everything they have in the house, including their own beds, free to a stranger, and frequently refusing payment for lodging or food.   They are also very honest ; crimes against property being of very rare occurrence.   The other day, a Northern gentleman visiting here expressed his fears of being robbed to a native farmer.   The latter, after inquiring whether there were any prisons and police in New England, what these were for, and whether his interrogator had locks to his own doors and safes and bars to his window-

shutters in Boston, remarked, " Wal, I've lived here
man and boy for forty year, and never had a bolt to
my house, or corn loft, or smoke-house ; and I'll tell
you what ; I'll give you a dollar for every lock you
can find in Scott county." The cattle, sheep, and
hogs wander perfectly unguarded through the forest,
and I have not yet heard of a single instance of a
stolen beast.

There is a rough water mill on a creek close by,
called Buck's Mill, which was run by the owner for
years—until he sold it a few months ago—on the following system : He put the running gear and stones
up, and above the latter a wooden box, with the charge
for grinding meal marked outside. He visited the mill
once a fortnight, looked to the machinery, and took
away whatever coin was in the box. Folks brought
their corn down the steep bank if they chose, ground
it at their leisure, and then, if they were honest, put
the fee in the box ; if not, they went off with their
meal, and a consciousness that they were rogues. I
presume Buck found his plan answer, as he pursued it
up to the date of sale.

In short, sir, I have been driven to the conclusion,
in spite of all traditional leanings the other way, that
the Lord has much people in these mountains, as I
think a young English deacon, lately ordained by the
Bishop of Tennessee, will find, who passed here yesterday on a buggy, with his young wife and child, and
two boxes and ten dollars of the goods of this world,
on his way to open a church mission in a neighbouring county. I heard yesterday a story which should
give him hope as to the female portion, at any rate,
of his possible flock. They are dreadful slatterns, with-

F

out an inkling of the great Palmerstonian truth that dirt is matter in its *wrong* place. A mountain girl, however, who had, strange to say, taken the fancy to go as housemaid in a Knoxville family, gave out that she had been converted. Doubts being expressed and questions asked as to the grounds on which she based this assurance, she replied that she knew it was all right because now she swept underneath the rugs.

When one gets on stories of quaint and ready replies in these parts, one " slops over on both shoulders." Here are a couple which are current in connection with the war, upon which, naturally enough, the whole mind of the people is still dwelling, being as much occupied with it as with their other paramount subject, the immediate future development of the unbounded resources of these States, which have been really opened for the first time by that terrible agency. An active Secessionist leader in a neighbouring county, in one of his stump speeches before the war had announced that the Southerners, and especially Tennessee mountain men, could whip the white-livered Yanks with popguns. Not long since, having been amnestied and reconstructed again to a point when he saw his way to running for a State office, he was reminded of this saying at the beginning of his canvass : " Wal, yes," he said, " I own to that, and I stand by it still, only those mean cusses [the Yanks] wouldn't fight that way."

The other is of a very different stamp, and will hold its own with many world-wide stories of graceful compliments to former enemies by kings and other bigwigs. General Wilder, one of the most successful and gallant of the Northern corps commanders in the war, has established himself in this State, with whose climate and resources he became so familiar in the campaign which ended under Look-out Mountain. He has built up a great iron industry at Chatanooga, in full sight of the battle-fields from which 14,000 bodies of Union soldiers were carried to the national cemetery. Early in his Chatanooga career he met one of the most famous of the Southern corps commanders (Forrest, I believe, but am not sure as to the name), who, on being introduced, said, " General, I have long wished to know you, because you have behaved to me in a way for which I reckon you owe me an apology as between gentlemen." Wilder replied in astonishment that to his knowledge they had never met before, but that he was quite ready to do all that an honourable man ought. "Well, now, General," said the other " you remember such and such a fight [naming it]. By night you had taken every gun I had, and I consider that quite an ungentlemanly advantage to take of a man anyhow."

By the way no man bears more frank testimony to the gallantry of the Southern soldiers than General Wilder, or admits more frankly the odds which the superior equipment of the Federals threw against the Confederate armies. His corps, mounted infantry armed with repeating rifles, were equal, he thinks, to at least three times their number of as good soldiers as themselves with the ordinary Southern arms. There are few pleasanter things to a hearty well-wisher, who has not been in America for ten years, than the change which has taken place in public sentiment, indicated by such frank admissions as the one just referred to. In 1870, any expression of admiration for the gallantry of the South, or of respect or appreciation of such men as Lee, Jackson, Longstreet, or Johnson, was received either silently or with strong disapproval. Now it is quite the other way, so far as I have seen as yet, and I cannot but hope that the last scars of the mighty struggle are healing up rapidly and thoroughly, and that the old sectional hatred and scorn lie six feet under ground, in the national cemeteries :—

> " No more shall the war-cry sever,
> 　Or the inland rivers run red ;
> We have buried our anger for ever,
> 　In the sacred graves of the dead.
>
> Under the sod and the dew,
> 　Waiting the Judgment-day ;
> Love and tears for the blue !
> 　Tears and love for the gray !"

No man can live for a few weeks on these Cumberland Mountains without responding with a hearty " Amen."

VACUUS VIATOR.

CHAPTER VI.

OUR FORESTER.

Nothing would satisfy our forester but that some of us should ride over with him, some nine miles through the forest, to see Glades, the farm upon which he has been for the last eight years. He led the way, on his yellow mare, an animal who had nearly given us sore trouble here. The head stableman turned all the horses out one day for a short run, and she being amongst them, and loving her old home best, went off straight for Glades through the woods, with every hoof after her. Luckily, Alfred, the forester's son, was there, and guessing what was the matter, just rode her back, all the rest following. The ride was lovely, glorious peeps of distant blue ranges, and the forest just breaking out all over into golds, and vermilions, and purples, and russets. We only passed two small farms on the way, both ramshackle, and so the treat of coming suddenly on some hundred acres cleared, drained, with large though rough farm buildings, and bearing the look of being cared for, was indescribably pleasant. Mrs. Hill and her son Alfred received us, both worthy of the head of the house; more I cannot say. They run the farm in his absence with scarcely any help, Alfred having also to attend to a grist and saw mill in the neigh-

bouring creek. There were a fine mare and filly in
the yard, as tame as pet dogs, coming and shoving
their noses into your pockets and coaxing you for
apples. The hogs are good Berkshire breed, the sheep
Cotswolds. The cows (it is the only place where we
have had cream on the mountains) Alderney or short-
horns. The house is a large log cabin, one big room, with
a deep open fireplace, where a great pine-log smouldered
at the back across plain iron dogs; a big hearth in
front, on which pitch-pine chips are thrown when you
feel inclined for a blaze. The room is carpeted and
hung with photographs and prints, a rifle and shot
gun, and implements of one kind or another. A small
collection of books, mostly theological, and founded on
two big Bibles; two rocking and half a dozen other
chairs, a table, and two beds in the corners farthest
from the fire, complete the furniture of the room, which
opens on one side on a deep verandah, and on the other
on a lean-to, which serves for kitchen and dining-room,
and ends in a small, spare bedroom. A loft above,
into which the family disappeared at night, completes
the accommodation. I need not dwell on our supper,
which included tender mutton, chickens, apple tart,
custard pudding, and all manner of vegetables and
cakes. Mrs. Hill is as notable a cook as her husband
is a forester. After supper we drew round the big fireplace, and soon prevailed on our host to give us a sketch
of his life, by way of encouragement to his three young
countrymen who sat round, and are going to try their
fortunes in these mountains :—

      " I was born and bred up in one of Lord Denbigh's
cottages, at Kirby, in Warwickshire. My father was
employed on the great place, that's Nuneham Paddocks,

you know. He was a labourer, and brought up sixteen
children, not one of whom, except me, has ever been
summonsed before a Justice, or got into any kind of
trouble. I went to school till about nine, but I was
always longing to be out in the fields at plough or bird-
keeping; so I got away before I could do much reading
or writing. But I kept on at Sabbath school, and learnt
more there than I did at t'other. The young ladies
used to teach, and they'd set us pieces and things to learn
for them in the week. ' My Cæsar ' [the only ejacula-
tion Amos allows himself; he cannot remember where
he picked it up], how I would work at my piece to get
it for Lady Mary ! I've fairly cried over it sometimes,
but I always managed to get it, somehow. After a bit,
I was taken on at the house. At first I did odd jobs,
like cleaning boots and carrying messages; and then I
got into the garden, and from that into the stable; and
then for a bit with the keepers; and then into livery,
to wait on the young ladies. So you see I learnt something of everything, and was happy and earning good
wages. But I wanted to see the world, so I took service with a gentleman who was a big railway contractor.
I used to drive him, and do anything a'most that he
wanted. I stayed with him nine years, and 'twas
while going about with him that I met my wife here.
We got married down in Kent, thirty-six years ago.
Yes [in answer to a laughing comment by his wife],
I wanted some one to mind me, in those days. That
poaching trouble came about this way. I had charge
for my master of a piece of railway that ran through
Lord ——'s preserves, in Wales. There were very strict
rules about trespassing on the lines then, because folks
there didn't like our line, and had been putting things

on it to upset the trains.   One day I saw two keepers
coming down the line, with a labourer I knew between
them.   He was all covered with blood from a wound
in his head.   'Why,' said I, 'what's the matter now?'
'I've been out of work,' he said, 'this three weeks, and
I was digging out a rabbit to get something to eat,
when they came up and broke my head.'   From that
time the keepers and I quarrelled.   I summonsed them,
and got them fined for trespassing on the line; and
then they got me fined for trespassing on their covers.
We watched one another like hawks.   I'd often lie out
at night for hours in the cold, in a ditch, where I knew
they'd want to cross the line, and then jump up and
catch them; and they'd do the same by me.   Once
they got me fined £3 : 10s. for poaching.   I remember
it well.   I was that riled, I said to the justices right
out, 'How long do you think it'll take me, gentlemen,
to pay all that money, with hares only 1s. a-piece?'
Then I went in for it.   I remembered the text, 'What
thy hand findeth to do, do it with thy might.'   I did it.
I used to creep along at night, all up the fences, and
feel for the places where the hares came through and
set my wires; and I'd often have ten great ones scream-
ing and flopping about like mad.   And that's what the
keepers were, too.   I've given a whole barrowful of hares
away to the poor folk of a morning.   Well, I know [in
answer to an interpellation of Mrs. Hill] yes, 'twas all
wrong, and I was a wild chap in those days.   Then I
began to hear talk about America, and all there was for a
man to see and do there, so I left my master, and we came
over, twenty-seven years ago.   At first I took charge
of gentlemen's gardens in New York and New Jersey.
Then we went to Michigan, where I could earn all I

wanted. Money was of no account there for a good
man in those days, but the climate was dreadful sickly,
and we had our baby, the first we had in twelve years,
and wanted to live on bread and water so as we could
save him. So we went up right amongst the Indians,
to a place they call Grand Travers, a wonderful healthy
place, on a lake in the pine-forest country, as it was
then. I went on to a promontory, where the forest
stood, not like it does here, but the trees that thick
you had scarce room to swing an axe. Well, it was a
beautiful healthy place, and we and baby throve, and I
soon made a farm; and then folk began to follow after
us; and before I left there were twenty-three saw-mills,
cutting up from 80,000 to 150,000 feet a day, week in
and out. They've stripped the country so now that
there's no lumber for those mills to cut, and most of
them have stopped. I used to have a boat, with just a
small sail, and I'd take my stuff down in the morning,
and trade it off to the lumber-men, and then sail back
at night, for the wind changed and blew back in the
evenings most part of the year. Well, then, the war
came, and for two years I kept thinking whether I
oughn't to do my part to help the Government I'd
lived under so long. Besides, I hated slavery. So in
the third year I made up my mind, and 'listed in the
Michigan Cavalry. I took the whole matter before
the Lord, and prayed I might do my duty as a soldier,
and not hurt any man. Well, we joined the Cavalry,
near 60,000 strong down in these parts; and I was
at Knoxville, and up and down. It was awful, the
language and the ways of the men—many of them at
least—swearing, and drinking, and stealing any kind of
thing they could lay hands on. Many's the plan for

stealing I've broken upon, telling them they were there
to sustain the flag, not to rob poor folks. I spoke very
plain all along, and got the men, many of them any
way, to listen. I got on famously, too, because I was
never away plundering, and my horse was always ready
for any service. An officer would come in, after we
had had a long day's work, to say a despatch or message must go, and no horse in our company was fit to
go but mine, so the orderly must have him; but I
always said no, I was quite ready to go myself, but
would not part company from my horse. The only
time I took what was not mine was when we surprised
a Confederate convoy, and got hold of the stores they
were carrying. There they were lying all along the
roads, greatcoats and blankets, and meal bags, and
good boots, with English marks on them. My Cæsar,
how our men were destroying them! I got together
a lot of the poor starving folk out of the woods that
both sides had been living on, and loaded them up
with meal and blankets. My Cæsar, how I loved to
scatter them English boots! They never had seen
such before. No, sir [in reply to one of us], I never
fired a shot all that time, but I had hundreds fired
at me. I've been in the rifle pits, and now and again
seen a fellow drawing a bead on me, and I'd duck down
and hear the bullet pinge into the bank close above.

" They got to employ me a good deal carrying de-
spatches and scouting. That's how I got took at last.
We were at a place called Strawberry Plains, with
Breckenbridge's Division pretty near all round us. I
was sent out with twelve other men, to try and draw
them out, to show their force and position; and so we
did, but they were too quick for us. Out they came,

and it was a race back to our lines down a steep creek.
My horse missed his footing, and down we rolled over
and over, into the water.   When I got up, I was up
to my middle, and, first thing I knew, there was a
rebel, who swore at me for a G——d d—— Yankee, and
fired his six-shooter at me.   The shot passed under
my arm, and, before he could fire again, an officer
ordered him on, and gave me in charge.   I was taken
to the rear, and marched off with a lot of prisoners.
The rebels treated me as if I'd been their father, after
a day or two.   I spoke out to them about their swearing and ways, just as I had to our men ; and I might
have been tight all the time I was a prisoner, only I'm
a temperance man.   They put me on their horses on
the march, and I was glad of it, for I was hurt by my
roll with my horse, and bad about the chest.   After
about six days I got my parole, with five others.   They
were hard pressed then, and didn't want us toting
along.   Then we started north, with nothing but just
our uniforms, and they full of vermin.   The first house
we struck I asked where we could find a Union man
about there.   They didn't know any one, didn't think
there was one in the county.   I said that was bad, as
we were paroled Union soldiers,——and then all was
changed.   They took us in and wanted us to use their
beds, which we wouldn't do, because of the vermin on
us.   They gave us all they had, and I saw the women,
for I couldn't sleep, covering us up with any spare
clothes they'd got, and watching us all night long.
They sent us on to other Union houses, and so we got
north.   I was too ill to stay north at my old work, so
I sold my farm and came south to Knoxville, where I
had come to know many kind, good people in the war.

They were very kind, and I got work at the improvements on Mr. Dickenson's farm (a model farm we had
gone over), and in other gentlemen's gardens.   But I
didn't get my health again, so eight years ago I came
to this place on the mountains, which I knew was
healthy, and would suit me.   Well, they all said I
should be starved out in two years and have to quit,
but before three years were out I was selling them
corn, and better bacon than they'd ever had before.
Some of 'em begin to think I'm right now, and there's
a deal of improvement going on, and if they'd only, as
I tell 'em, just put in all their time on their farms,
and not go loafing round gunning, contented with corndodgers and a bit of pork, and give up whisky, they
might all do as well as I've done.   I should like to go
back once more and see the old country ; but I mean
to end my days here.   There's no such country that
I ever saw.   The Lord has done all for us here.   And
it seems like dreams that I should live to see a Rugby
up here on the mountains.   I mean to take a lot in
the town, or close by, and call it Nuneham Paddocks.
So I shall lay my bones, you see, in the same place,
as it were, that I was reared in."

I do not pretend that these were his exact words,
——the whole had to be condensed to come within your
space, but they are not far off.   It was now past nine,
the time for retiring, when Amos told us that he
always ended his day with family prayers.   A psalm
was read, and then we knelt down, and he prayed for
some minutes.   Extempore prayers always excite my
critical faculty, but there was no thought or expression
in this I could have wished to alter.   Then we turned
in, I, after a pipe in the verandah, in one clean white
bed, and two of the boys in the big one in the oppo-

site corner.　There I soon dozed off, watching the big, smouldering white pine-log away in the depth of the chimney-nook, and the last flickerings of the knobs of pitch-pine in front of it, between the iron dogs, and wondering in my mind over the brave story we had just been listening to, so simply told (of which I fear I have succeeded in giving a very poor reflection), and whether there are not some—there cannot, I fear, be many—such lives lying about in out-of-the-way corners, of mountain, or plain, or city.　My last conscious speculation was whether, after all, the Union would have been saved if all Union soldiers had been Amos Hills.

I waked early, just before dawn, and was watching alternately the embers of the big log, still aglow in the deep chimney, and the white light beginning to break through the honeysuckles and vines which hung over the verandah, and shaded the wide-open window, when the clock struck five.　The door opened softly, and in stepped Amos Hill in his stockings.　He came to the foot of our beds, picked up our dirty boots, and stole out again as noiselessly as he had entered.　The next minute I heard the blacking brushes going vigorously, and knew that I should appear at breakfast with a shine on in which I should have reason to glory, if I were preparing to walk in Bond Street, instead of through the scrub on the Cumberland Mountains.　I turned over for another hour's sleep (breakfast being at 6.30 sharp), but not without first considering for some minutes which of us two—if things were fixed up straight in this blundering old world—ought to be blacking the other's boots.　The conclusion I came to was that it ought *not* to be Amos Hill.

VACUUS VIATOR.

CHAPTER VII.

THE NEGRO "NATIVES."

RUGBY, TENNESSEE.

THERE is one inconvenience in this desultory mode of correspondence,—that one is apt to forget what one has told already, and to repeat oneself. I have written something of the white native of these mountains; have I said anything of his dark brother? The subject is becoming a more and more interesting and important one every day, through all these regions. In these mountains, the negro, perhaps, can scarcely be called a native. Very few black families, I am told, were to be found here a year or two since. My own eyes assure me that they are multiplying rapidly. I see more and more black men amongst the gangs on roads and bridges, and come across queer little encampments in the woods, with a pile of logs smouldering in the midst, round which stand the mirth-provoking figures of small black urchins, who stare and grin at the intruder on horseback, till he rides on under the gold and russet and green autumnal coping of hickories, chestnuts, and pines.

I am coming to the conclusion that wherever work is to be had, in Tennessee, at any rate, there will the negro be found. He seems to gather to a contractor like the buzzards, which one sees over the tree-tops, to

carrion. And unless the white natives take to "putting
in all their time," whatever work is going will not
long remain with them. The negro will loaf and shirk
as often as not when he gets the chance, but he has not
the white craving for knocking off altogether as soon as
he has a couple of dollars in his pocket; has no strong
hunting instinct; and has not acquired the art of letting
his pick drop listlessly into the ground with its own
weight, and stopping to admire the scenery after every
half-dozen strokes.

The negro is much more obedient, moreover, and
manageable,—obedient to a fault, if one can believe
the many stories one hears of his readiness to commit
small misdemeanours and crimes, and not always small
ones, at the bidding of his employers. There is one
thing, however, which an equally unanimous testimony
agrees in declaring that he will not do, and that is, sell
his vote, or be dragooned into giving it for any one but
his own choice; he may, indeed, be scared from voting,
but cannot be " squared ;" a singular testimony, surely,
of his prospective value as a citizen.

Equally strong is the evidence of his resolute determination to get his children educated. In some Southern
States the children are, I believe, kept apart, but in the
only mountain school I have had the chance of seeing,
black and white children were together. They were not
in class, but in the front of the barn-like building used
both for church and school, having just come out for
the dinner-hour. There was a large, sandy, trampled
place under the trees, by no means a bad play-ground,
on which a few of the most energetic, the blacks in the
majority, were playing at some game as we came up, the
mysteries of which I should have liked to study. But the

longer we stayed the less chance there seemed of their
going on, and the game remains a mystery to me still.
Where these children, some fifty in number, came from,
is a problem; but there they were from somewhere.
And everywhere, I hear, the blacks are forcing the
running with respect to education, and great numbers
of them are showing a thrift and energy which are
likely to make them formidable competitors in the
struggle for existence, at any rate in all States south
of Kentucky.

In one department (a very small one, no doubt), they
will have crowded out the native whites in a very short
time, if I may judge by our experience in this house.
We number two ladies and six men, and our whole
service is done by one boy.   Our first experiment was
with a young native, who " reared up " on the first
morning at the idea of having to black boots.   This
prejudice, I think I told you, was removed for the
moment, and he stayed for a few days.   Where it was
he "weakened on us" I could not learn for certain, but
incline to the belief that it was either having to carry
the racquets and balls to the lawn-tennis ground, or to
get a fire to burn in order to boil the water for a four
o'clock tea.   Both these services were ordered by the
ladies, and I thought I saw signs (though I am far
from certain) that his manly soul rose against feminine
command.   Be that as it may, off he went without
warning, and soon after Amos Hill arrived, with almost
pathetic apologies and a negro boy, short of stature,
huge of mouth, fabulous in the apparent age of his
garments, named Jeff.   He had no other name, he told
us, and did not know whether it signified Jefferson or
Geoffrey, or where or how he got it, or anything about

himself, except that he had got our place at $5 a month,
—at which he showed his ivory, " some ! "

From this time all was changed. Jeff, it is true,
after the first two days, gave proofs that he was not
converted, like the white housemaid who had learned
to sweep under the mats. His sweeping and tidying
were decidedly those of the sinner ; and he entirely
abandoned the only hard work we set him, as soon as
it was out of sight from the asylum. It was a path
leading to a shallow well, which the boys had dug at
the bottom of the garden. The last twenty yards or
so are on a steeper incline than the part next the
house : so Jeff studiously completed the piece in sight
of the house, and never put pick or shovel on the
remainder, which lay behind the friendly brow of the
slope. But in all other directions, where the work
was mainly odd jobs, a respectable kind of loafing, Jeff
was always to the fore, acquitting himself to the best,
I think, of his ability.

We did not get full command of him till the arrival
of a young Texan cattle-driver, who taught us the
peculiar cry for the negro, by appending a high " Ho "
to his name, or rather running them together, so that
the whole sounded " Hojeff ! " as nearly as possible one
syllable. Even the ladies picked up the cry, and
thenceforward Jeff's substitute for the " Anon, anon,
sir ! " of the Elizabethan waiter was instantaneous. He
built a camp-oven, like those of the Volunteers at
Wimbledon, and neater of construction, from which he
supplied a reasonably constant provision of hot water
from 6 A.M., of course cutting his own logs for the
fire. His highest achievement was ironing the ladies'
cotton dresses, which they declared he did not very

badly. Most of us entrusted him with the washing
of flannel shirts and socks, which at any rate were
faithfully immersed in suds, and hung up to dry under
our eyes. The laundry was an army tent, pitched at
the back of the asylum, where Jeff spent nearly all
his time when not under orders, generally munching
an apple, of which there was always a sack lying
about, a present from some ranch-owner, or brought
over from the garden, and open to mankind at large.
I never could find out whether he could read. One
evening he came up proudly to ask whether " his mail "
had come, and sure enough when the mail arrived
there was a post-card, which he claimed. We thought
he would ask one of us to read it for him, but were
disappointed. He had a habit of crooning over and
over again all day some scrap of a song. One of these
excited my curiosity exceedingly, but I never succeeded
in getting more than two lines out of him,——

" Oh my ! oh my ! I've got a hundred dollars in a mine ! "

One had a crave to hear what came of those hundred
dollars. It seems it is so almost universally. The nearest approach to a complete negro ditty which I have
been able to strike is one which the Texan gives, with
a wonderful roll of the word " chariot," which cannot
be expressed in print. It runs :——

> The Debble he chase me round a stump,
>   Gwine for to carry me home ;
> He grab for me at ebery jump,
>   Gwine for to carry me home.
> Swing low, sweet *cha-y-ot*.
>   Gwine for to carry me home.
>
> The Debble he make one grab at me,
>   Gwine, etc.

> He missed me, and my soul goed free,
>   Gwine, etc.
> Swing low, etc.
>
> Oh ! wun't we have a gay old time,
>   Gwine, etc.
> A eatin' up o' honey, and a drinkin' up o' wine.
>   Gwine, etc.
> Swing low, etc.

This, Sir, I think you will agree with me, though precious, is obviously a fragment only. It took our Texan many months to pick it up, even in this mutilated condition.

But, after all, Jeff's character and capacity come out most in the direction of boots. It is from his attitude with regard to them that I incline to think that the Black race have a great future in these States. You may have gathered from previous letters that there is a clear, though not a well marked, division in this settlement as to blacking. Amos Hill builds on it decidedly, and would have every farmer appear in blacked boots, at any rate on Sunday. The opposition is led by a young farmer of great energy and famous temper, who, having been "strapped," or left without a penny, three hundred miles from the Pacific coast, amongst the Mexican mines, and having made his hands keep his head in the wildest of earthly settlements, has a strong contempt for all amenities of clothing, which is shared by the geologist and others. How the point will be settled at last I cannot guess. It stands over while the ladies are still here, and I have actually seen the "strapped" one giving his wondrous boots a sly lick or two of blacking on Sunday morning.

But, anyhow, the blacks will be cordially on the

side of polish and the aristocracy. This one might
perhaps have anticipated; but what I was not prepared for was Jeff's apparent passion for boots. I
own a fine strong pair of shooting-boots, which he
worshipped for five minutes at least every morning.
As my last day in the asylum drew on I could see
he was troubled in his mind. At last, out it came.
Watching his chance, when no one was near, he sidled
up, and pointing to them on the square chest in the
verandah which served for blacking-board, he said,
" I'd like to buy dem boots." After my first astonishment was over, I explained to him that I couldn't
afford to sell them for less than about six weeks of his
wages, and that, moreover, I wanted them for myself,
as I could get none such here. He was much disappointed, and muttered frequently, " I'd like to buy
dem boots ! " but my heart did not soften.

Perhaps I ought rather to be giving your readers
more serious experiences, but somehow the negro is
apt to run one out into chaff. However, I will conclude with one fact, which seems to me a very striking
confirmation of my view. All Americans are reading
the *Fool's Errand*, a powerful novel, founded on the
state of things after the war in the Kuklux times. It
is written by a Southern Judge, obviously a fair and
clever man, but one who has no more faith in the
negro's power to raise himself to anything above hew-
ing wood and drawing water for the " Caucasian " than
Chief-Justice Taney himself. In all that book there is
no instance of the drawing of a mean, corrupt, or
depraved negro ; but they are represented as full of
patience, trustfulness, shrewdness, and power of many
kinds.   VACUUS VIATOR.

CHAPTER VIII.

RUGBY, TENNESSEE.

OUR opening day drew near, not without rousing the most serious misgivings in the minds of most of us whether we could possibly be ready to receive our guests. Invitations had been issued to our neighbours— friends, as we had learnt to esteem them— in Cincinnati, Knoxville, Chatanooga, whose hospitalities we had enjoyed, and who had expressed a cordial sympathy with our enterprise, and a desire to visit us. We looked also for some of our own old members from distant New England, in all probability seventy or eighty guests, to lodge and board, and convey from and back to the railway, seven miles over our new road,—no small undertaking, under our circumstances. But the hotel was still in the hands of the contractor, from whom, as yet, only the upper floors had been rescued. The staircase wanted banisters, and the hall and living-rooms were still only half-wainscoted, and full of carpenters' benches and plasterers' trays ; while the furniture and crockery lumbered up the big barn, or stood about in cases on the broad verandah. As for our road, it was splendid, so far as it went, but some two miles were still merely a forest track, from which all trees and stumps had been removed, but that was all. The bridge, too, over the Clear Fork stream, by which the town site is entered, had only the first cross-timbers laid from pier to pier, while the approaches seemed to lie in hopeless weltering confusion, difficult on horseback, impossible on wheels. However, the manager declared that we should drive over the bridge on Saturday afternoon, and that the contractor should be out of the hotel by Monday mid-day. With this we were obliged to be content, though it was running things fine, as we looked for our guests on that Monday afternoon, and the opening was fixed for the next morning. However, as the manager said, so it came to pass. Bridge and road were declared passable by the named time, though nervous persons may well have thought twice before attempting the former in the heavy omnibuses hired for the occasion ; and we were able to get possession, and move furniture and crockery into the hotel, though the carpenters still held the unfinished staircase.

So far, so good; but still everything, we felt, depended on the weather. If the glorious days we had been having held, all would be well. The promise was fair up to Sunday evening, but at sunset there was a change. Amos Hill shook his head, and the geologist's aneroid barometer gave ominous signs. They proved only too correct. Early in the night the rain set in, and by daybreak, when we were already astir, a steady, soft, searching rain was coming down perpendicularly, which lasted, with scarcely a break, clear through the day, and till midnight. With feelings of blank despair we thought of the new road, softened into a Slough of Despond, and the hastily thrown-up approaches to the bridge giving way under the laden omnibuses, and

waited our fate.   It was, as usual, better than we
looked for.   The morning train from Chatanooga would
bring our southern guests in time for early dinner, if
no break-down happened; and sure enough, within half-
an-hour of the expected time, up came the omnibuses,
escorted to the hotel door by the manager and his son,
on horseback; and the Bishop of Tennessee, with his
chaplain, the Mayor of Chatanooga, and a number of
the leading citizens of that city and of Knoxville, de-
scended in the rain.   In five minutes we were at our
ease and happy.   If they had all been Englishmen on
a pleasure-trip, they could not have taken the down-
pour more cheerily as a matter of course, and pleasant,
rather than otherwise, after the long drought.   They
dined, chatted, and smoked .in the verandah, and then
trotted off in *gum* coats to look round at the walks,
gardens, streets, and buildings, escorted by "the boys."
The manager reported, with pride, that they had come
up in an hour and a quarter, and without any kind of
contretemps, though, no doubt, the new road *was* deep
in places.

All anxiety was over for the moment, as the northern
train, bringing our Cincinnati and New-England friends,
was not due till after dark.   We sat down to tea in
detachments from six to eight, when, if all went well,
the northerners would be about due.   The tables were
cleared, and relaid once more for them, and every preparation made to give them a warm welcome.   Nine
struck, and still no sign of them ; then ten, by which
time, in this early country, all but some four or five
anxious souls had retired.   We sat round the stove in
the hall, and listened to the war stories of the Mayor
of Chatanooga, and our host of the Tabard, who had

served on opposite sides in the terrible campaigns in
the south of this State, which had ended at Missionary
Ridge, and filled the national cemetery of Chatanooga
with 14,000 graves of Union soldiers.   But neither
the interest of the stories themselves, nor the pleasure
of seeing how completely all bitterness had passed out
of the narrators' minds, could keep our thoughts from
dwelling on the pitch-dark road, sodden by this time
with the rain, and the *mauvais pas* of the bridge.

Eleven struck, and now it became too serious for
anything but anxious peerings into the black night, and
considerations as to what could be done.   We had
ordered lanterns, and were on the point of starting for the
bridge, when faint sounds, as of men singing in chorus
came through the darkness.   They grew in volume,
and now we could hear the omnibuses, from which
came a roll of "John Brown's body lies mouldering in
the grave," given with a swing and precision which
told of old campaigners.   That stirring melody could
hardly have been more welcome to the first line waiting
for supports, on some hard-fought battle-ground, than it
was to us.   The omnibuses drew up, a dense cloud rising
from the drenched horses and mules, and the singers
got out, still keeping up their chorus, which only ceased
on the verandah, and must have roused every sleeper
in the settlement.   The Old Bay State, Ohio, and Kentucky had sent us a set of as stalwart good fellows as
ever sang a chorus or ate a beefsteak at midnight ; and
while they were engaged in the latter operation they
told how, from the breakdown of a freight-train on
the line, theirs had been three hours late ; how the
darkness had kept them to a foot's-pace ; how the last
omnibus had given out in the heavy places, and had to

be constantly helped on by a pair of mules detached
from one of the others. "All's well that ends well,"
and it was with a joyful sense of relief that we piloted
such of our guests as the hotel could not hold across to
their cots in the barracks at one in the morning. By
nine, the glorious southern sun had fairly vanquished
rain and mist, and the whole plateau was ablaze with
the autumn tints, and every leaf gleaming from its
recent shower-bath. Rugby outdid herself, and "leapt
to music and to light" in a way which astonished even
her oldest and most enthusiastic citizens, some half-
dozen of whom had had nearly twelve months' experience of her moods and tempers. Breakfast began at
six, and ended at nine, and for three hours batches of
well-fed visitors were turned out to saunter round the
walks, the English gardens, and lawn-tennis grounds,
until the hour of eleven, fixed by the bishop for the
opening service. The church being as yet only some
six feet above ground, this ceremony was to be held in
the verandah of the hotel. Meantime, bishop and chaplain were busy among "the boys," organising a choir to
sing the hymns and lead the responses. The whole
population were gathering round the hotel, some four
or five buggies, and perhaps twenty horses haltered to
the nearest trees, showed the interest excited in the
neighbourhood. In addition to the seats in the verandah, chairs and benches were placed on the ground
below for the surplus congregation, behind whom a
fringe of white and black natives regarded the proceedings with grave attention. Punctual to time, the
bishop and his chaplain, in robes, took their places at
the corner of the verandah, and gave out the first verses
of the "Old Hundredth." There was a moment's pause,

while the newly-organised choir exchanged glances as to
who should lead off, and the pause was fatal to them.
For on the bishop's left stood the stalwart New-Eng-
lander who had led the pilgrims of the previous evening
in the " John Brown " chorus.   He, unaware of the
episcopal arrangements, and of the consequent vested
rights of " the boys," broke out with, " All people that
on earth do dwell," in a voice which carried the whole
assembly with him, and at once reduced " the boys," to
humble followers.   They had their revenge, however,
when it came to the second hymn at the end of the
service.   It was " Jerusalem, the golden," which is
apparently sung to a different tune in Boston to that in
use in England ; so, though our musical guest struggled
manfully through the first line, and had almost discom-
fited "the boys" by sheer force of lungs, numbers pre-
vailed, and he was brought into line.

The service was a short one, consisting of two psalms,
"Lord, who shall dwell in thy tabernacle?" and "Except
the Lord build the house," the chapter of Solomon's
prayer at the dedication of the Temple, half a dozen of
the Church collects, and a prayer by the bishop that
the town and settlement might be built up in righteous-
ness and the fear and love of God, and prove a blessing
to the State.   Then, after the blessing, the gathering
resolved itself into a public meeting after American
fashion.   The Board spoke through their representatives, and bishop, judge, general manager, and visitors
exchanged friendly oratorical buffets, and wishes and pro-
phecies for the prosperity of " the New Jerusalem " in
the southern highlands.   A more genuine or healthier
act of worship it has not been our good fortune to attend
in these late years.

Dinner began immediately afterwards, and then the company scattered again, some to select town lots, some to the best views, the bishop to organise a vestry, and induce two of "the boys" to become lay readers, pending the arrival of a parson (in which he was eminently successful); the chaplain to the Clear Fork, with one of the boys' fishing-rods, after black bass; and a motley crowd to the lawn-tennis ground, to see some sets played which would have done no discredit to Wimbledon, and excited much wonder and some enthusiasm amongst natives and visitors.   A cheerful evening followed, in which the new piano in the hotel sitting-room did good service, and many war and other stories were told round the big hall stove.   Early the next morning the omnibuses began carrying off the visitors, and by night Rugby had settled down again to its ordinary life, not, however, without a sense of strength gained for the work of building up a community which shall know how to comport itself in good and bad times, and shall help, instead of hindering, its sons and daughters in leading a brave, simple, and Christian life.—I am, Sir, etc.

VACUUS VIATOR.

PART III.

BOARD OF AID TO LAND OWNERSHIP.

OPENING THE TOWN SITE OF RUGBY,
OCTOBER 5, 1880.

CHAPTER I.

ADDRESS OF THE PRESIDENT.

I AM anxious to take this opportunity—the first public one I have had—to remove an impression which seems to have got abroad, that the settlement we are planting on these mountains and opening to-day is intended to be an English colony in a somewhat exclusive sense. Nothing can be further from the wishes and intentions of the founders. In a sense it is an English colony, no doubt, because at present all the settlers are English; but we hope that this will very soon cease to be so. Our settlement is open to all who like our principles and our ways, and care to come here to make homes for themselves: freely, without reserve or condition of any kind which does not bind us English also. Although the majority of us—the members of this board—are English, we have already amongst us a large, and I am happy to say an increasing number of American citizens. Leading men, not only in Boston—where the enterprise was first undertaken—but in New York, Philadelphia, and Cincinnati belong to us, and are as earnest and active in the work as any of our English members. They are as firmly convinced as we, that the future of our own race; and indeed of the world, in which our race is so clearly destined to play the leading part; can never be what it should be, until the most cordial alliance, the most intimate relations, have been established firmly, without any risk or possibility of disturbance or misunderstanding between its two great branches. We know of no way in which this can be brought about better than by such efforts as this we are making, in which Englishmen and Americans can stand shoulder to shoulder, and work with one mind and one heart for the same great end. If we knew of any such better ways we would gladly exchange our own for them.

These, then, are our views, which we have already endeavoured to express on more than one occasion in this State. And here let me take the opportunity of expressing our cordial thanks for, and appreciation of, the more than friendly spirit with which we have been met here, in our adopted home of Eastern Tennessee. We have been the guests already, by special invitation, of the citizens of Chattanooga and Knoxville, and have received invitations from Memphis, Nashville, and Louisville, which we greatly regret not to have been able to accept. In short, we have on all sides met not only with a lavish and thoughtful hospitality, but with assurances of sympathy and cordial understanding and appreciation, which have gone far to strengthen our purpose and remove all fears of failure in this mountain home, where we are trying our 'prentice hands on problems which we shall need all the strength and all

the wisdom we can get hold of to solve satisfactorily.
And while expressing our thanks, let me add my own
confident belief that our kind neighbours, many of whom
I trust are here to-day, will not find any reason to regret the frank and generous welcome which they have
given to a band of strangers.

And now, turning to the business on hand, let me
say, at least for myself, that I do not know how any
group of men and women, gathered together to-day in
any part of the world, can be engaged in a more ab-
sorbingly interesting, or indeed in a more responsible,
and I will add solemn, work than that to which I hope
most of us have now made up our minds to put our
hands earnestly, here, in this place, at this time.   For
we are about to open a town here—in other words, to
create a new centre of human life, human interests,
human activities—in this strangely beautiful solitude ;
a centre in which, as we trust, a healthy, hopeful,
reverent, or in one word godly, life shall grow up from
the first, and shall spread itself, so we hope, over all
the neighbouring region of these southern highlands.
Now surely, just to put this idea into words ought to
be enough to sober the spirits and brace up the energies
of the lightest-hearted and strongest amongst us.   He
to whom the work does not commend itself in this light
had better not put his hand to it at all in this place.

We are here, then, to-day—in this year 1880—
as pioneers; following, I hope and believe, as true an
instinct, or I should rather say as true a call, as any
that has been leading our fathers across the Atlantic to
this land of promise for the last quarter of a millennium.
There seem to be as clear indications now, as in the
early years of the seventeenth century, in the political

and social conditions of all the old settled nations
of Christendom——and in none more than our own
England——that this is a swarming time of the race ; a
time of great movements of population, which no human
power can check, but which may be either left to work
themselves out by rule of thumb, without intelligent
direction and guidance, or ordered and directed from
the first on distinct principles.   Well, those who are
interested in this enterprise have no doubt as to which
of these alternatives is to be preferred.   We are to do
our best to organise our infant community on such
lines and principles as our own experience and observation, and the study of the efforts of those who have
gone before us, seem to point out as the right and true
ones.

Well, then, how are we to set about this great
work ?   What is to be our starting-point ?   What the
idea which we are to try to realise ?   This is our first
need.   We must spare no pains to clear our minds on
this point.   Unless we do so, we shall get no coher-
ence and consistency in our later efforts.   We shall be
pulling different ways, and building up a Babel and
not a community, which sooner or later will share the
fate of all Babels, which the Lord will come down and
scatter abroad.   In this search, then, let us see whether
the word I have already used will not give us our clue.
We want to establish a *community*.   What does that
imply ?   This much, at any rate, that we should all
have *something* in common ; that we should recognise
some bond which binds us all together, and endeavour,
each and all of us, to keep this in view, to strengthen it
in all ways.   But what bond——what is it to be that those
who come to live here are to have in common ?   This

word community has gained an unenviable character in
our day.   We can scarcely think of a community
without coming upon the traces of those who have kept
and are keeping the Old World in a state of dangerous
distrust and alarm, and even in the New World have
given some ominous signs of sinister life.   Certainly
we can all agree at once that we have no sympathy
whatever with the state communism of Europe, represented by Lasalle and Karl Marx, and on this continent
by very inferior, and even more violent and anarchic,
persons.   We have no vision whatever to realise of a
paternal state, the owner of all property, finding easy
employment and liberal maintenance for all citizens,
reserving all profits for the community, and paying no
dividends to individuals.   Again, while respecting the
motives and lives of many of those who have founded
or are carrying on communistic experiments here and
in Europe, we have no desire or intention to follow in
their steps.   We are content with the laws relating to
private property and family life as we find them, feeling quite able to modify them for ourselves in certain
directions as our corporate conscience ripens, and becomes impatient of some of the evils which have
resulted from that overstrained desire of possession and
worship of possessions which marks our day.   But it
is time to leave negation and to get upon positive
ground.   As a community, we must have something in
common.   What is it to be, and how are we going to
treat it ?

Well, in the first place, there is this lovely corner
of God's earth which has been intrusted to us.   What,
as a community, is our first duty with regard to it ?
There can be no hesitation about the answer.   It is, to

treat it lovingly and reverently.　We can add little,
perhaps, to its natural beauty, but at least we can be
careful to spoil it as little as possible.　We may take
care that our children, or whoever our successors may
be here, shall not have cause to say—"See what a
glorious chance those old fellows had when they came
here in 1880, and how they threw it away!　This
town might have been the most beautiful on this continent, and look what they made of it!"

How, then, are we going to treat our site, so that
this reproach may never follow our memories?　First
as to the laying out of our town here.　We must do
this with a view to the common good, and with care
that neither convenience nor beauty is neglected.　And
as the guiding rule we may start with this, that there
shall be ample provision for all public wants from the
first.　We have here two beautiful streams which will
be a delight for ever to those who dwell here, if they
are left free for the use and enjoyment of all.　Therefore, in laying out the town we have reserved a strip of
various widths along the banks, which will remain
common property, and along which we hope to see
walks and rides carefully laid out, and kept in order
by the municipal authorities.　We have already in a
rough way, made a beginning by carrying a ride
along the banks of the Clear Fork and White Oak
Streams.　Then there must be reservations for parks,
gardens, and recreation grounds.　In the present
plans, provision has been made for these purposes.
There is Beacon Hill, the highest point, from which
there is a view of the whole surrounding country such
as few towns in the old or new world can boast.
This also will be common property, and the English

H

gardens, lawn tennis, and cricket ground, whenever the municipality are able to take them off the hands of the Board. What, if anything more is required, I hope we may consider and determine at once, and I can assure you that the Board is anxious to consult with, and meet the wishes of, those who propose to make homes here. Our wish is to preserve the natural beauties of this place for the people who live and visit here, and make them a constant means of educating the eye and mind. With this example and ideal before their eyes, we may hope that the lots which pass into the hands of private owners will also be handled with an eye to the common good. Private property must be, of course, fenced in, but the fences may surely be made with some regard to others than the owners. It is hoped that the impervious walls and fences, so common in England, may be avoided, and that, in dealing with lawns and trees, we may each of us bear his part in producing a beautiful picture.

Next comes the question of buildings, and here we must bear in mind that these are, in fact, or should be, the expression in timber, brick, and stone, of the thought of men and women as to the external conditions under which folk should live. Consider for a moment the different impressions in this matter which the visitor carries away from the streets of Chester, or Wells, or Salisbury, and from those of a town in our manufacturing districts. Now we hope that from the first visitors will carry away from this place the feeling that we here have understood something of what homes should be. Of course we must act prudently and cut our coats according to our cloth. We have no money to spare for superfluous decoration, and our

first buildings, both public and private, must be simple
and even rough in materials and construction.   But
there is no reason whatever why they should not, at
the same time, be sightly and good in form and proportion.   And at this I hope we shall all aim.

We shall try to set you a good example in the
public buildings.   These will consist, in the first
instance, of a church and school house, and then of a
court-house and town-hall, which will be built as soon
as we can see our way to doing so prudently, and can
make arrangements with the Government of the State
for our establishment as a county town.   We shall also
promote, so far as we can, good habits in this matter
of building, by providing plans and models of houses
of different sizes, such as we think will suit the site,
and do us credit as a community.   Of course every
man will build his house according to his own fancy,
and use it for whatever purpose he pleases, except for
the sale of intoxicating liquors, which will be strictly
prohibited ; but if, as a community, we can guide his
fancy in certain directions, we shall be glad, and consider that we have done good service.

So far, then, I hope, we have travelled the same
road without disagreement.   We shall be all of one
mind, I think, as to the preservation of all natural
beauty here in the treatment of grounds and buildings ;
and the sense of a common interest and life which an
ample provision of public buildings and grounds will
secure to our community.

Shall I carry you with me in the next step ?
Hitherto we have been concerned only in the first and
most necessary work of housing ourselves, but now, we
have to ask whether, after we are housed, and living in

our houses, the idea of a common life and common
interests must cease, and the isolated struggle for
existence, in which every man's hand will be for himself and against his neighbour, must begin.   The sur-
vival of the fittest is recognised as a natural law, which
means that men will always live upon, and not for,
one another.   Are we prepared to accept it uncon-
ditionally, or to try how far it can be modified by reason
and agreement ?   I, myself, have no doubt that it can
and ought to be so modified, and that we have a good
opportunity here for making the attempt.   And there
is, fortunately, no question as to the direction which
that effort should take in the first instance.

We have all of us a number of imperative wants
which must be provided for and satisfied day by day.
We want food, clothes, furniture, and a great variety
of things besides, which our nurture and culture have
made all but essential to us.   These must all be
provided here, either by each of us for himself, or by
some common machinery.   Well, we believe that it
can be done best by a common machinery, in which
we should like to see every one take a hand.   We
have a " commissary " already established, and have
used that word rather than " store " to indicate our
own wishes and intentions, as a " commissary " is especially a public institution.   Our wish is to make this
commissary a centre of supply, and that every settler,
or, at any rate, every householder here, should become
a member and part owner of it.   The machinery by
which this can be done is perfectly familiar in England.
If it is adopted, the cost price of establishing the present commissary, as it stands, will be divided into
small shares of five dollars each, so that the poorest

settler may not be inconvenienced by the outlay for membership. Every one will get whatever profits are made on his own consumption, and the business will be directed and superintended by a board or council chosen by the members themselves. In this way again we shall have a common interest and common property, and in the supplying of our own daily wants shall feel that if one member suffers, all suffer; if one rejoices, all rejoice. In this way, too, if we please, we may be rid once for all of the evils which have turned retail trade into a keen and anxious and, generally, a dishonest scramble in older communities: rid of adulteration, of false pretences, of indebtedness, of bankruptcy. Trade has been a potent civiliser of mankind, but only so far and so long as it has been kept in its place as a servant. As a master and an idol, it has proved a destroyer in the past, like all other idolatries, and is proving itself so in the present in many places we know of. Let us, as a community, take hold of it and master it here from the first, and never release our grasp and control of it.

There is another direction in which like common action may be taken at once. The company will for many years own large tracts of land round the town site which are well adapted to raising and pasturing cattle. We intend to establish this industry here at once, and desire to do so on the same lines as those already indicated with respect to the commissary. When it has been settled, therefore, what amount of capital will be required to make the experiment on the most favourable conditions, settlers will be invited to subscribe in small shares for such portion as they please, and the balance will be taken by the company.

The common herd will be managed by a committee elected by the shareholders. It is probable that considerable difficulty may occur in managing a large herd in this country, but the experiment can be made gradually and at once, and the Board are ready to give all the help in their power.

As time goes on, many other openings of a like kind may occur, but these will, for the present, be sufficient to establish and keep alive the corporate feeling, which is the main strength of all healthy communities.

If any of you should doubt whether such arrangements as these will not interfere with, and dwarf, the energy and enterprise of an infant community, and keep from it the ablest and most vigorous kind of men, I would submit that there will be full scope for all energy in other directions. No doubt there is a healthy and worthy rivalry which should exist in every community; but surely this may well be satisfied in the development of the numberless productive industries for which this region offers so wide a field. Who shall grow the best corn, tobacco, fruit; who shall raise the best stock on their own farms; produce the best articles, be they what they may; write the best books or articles; teach best, govern best; in a word, live most nobly,—surely here may well be scope enough for all energy, without the rivalry of shop-keeping, and the tricks of trade,—the adulteration, puffing and feverish meannesses which follow too surely in its train.

I must take you yet one step higher, and then I have done. Hitherto, we have been dealing with the outside only of our lives here, and questioning how far the idea of a community can be healthily realised in relation to these visible material things which we can

see and taste and handle. But we all know, and
confess to ourselves, if not to others, that no success
in dealing with or handling these can satisfy us as
men—or at any rate ought to satisfy us—that we are
one and all in contact with and living in a world in
which we have to do with other things than those
which rust and moth can corrupt. But here at once,
it may be urged, we are fighting against the *Zeit Geist*
—the spirit of our time—nowhere so strong and so
decided as here in America—if we make any effort to
deal as a community with the invisible. Here, at any
rate, we may be told, experience speaks emphatically
that men must be left free to follow the guidings of
their own consciences. You may possibly succeed, we
may be told, in supplying the material wants of all
by one central organisation started at once, but the
spiritual wants you will leave, if you are wise, to find
their own satisfaction, and to develop in such directions
and by such methods as chance may determine.

Now let me say at once, and with emphasis, that
there will be no attempt here to interfere with individual freedom. Every one will be free to worship in
his own way, and to provide for whatever religious
ministrations he requires, out of his own funds, and
according to his own ideas. But, this being granted,
is there not still something which we *may* profitably
attempt as a community ? We think there is, and
have accordingly appropriated certain lots as a means
of supporting public worship and religious ministrations here.

We are putting up a temporary building as a
church, in which the experiment will be tried whether
the members of different Christian denominations can

not agree well enough to use one building for their several acts of worship. In it, I trust, there will always be heard the Common Prayer of that Liturgy, which both in England and America has proved itself the best expression through many generations of the joys, hopes, and aspirations of a large portion of those who speak our language, and has risen from innumerable gatherings all round the globe laden with confessions of our shortcomings, and appeals for guidance and strength in the mighty work which has been laid upon our race.

I am, personally, not without hope that the meaning, and beauty, and value of common prayers will commend themselves to our community, and that all our citizens may learn to feel their pathos and their grandeur, and to use them with comfort and profit, though they may not be members of the National Church of England, or of the Episcopal Church of this country. But, as there will undoubtedly be also a desire for other forms of worship in which more direct expression can be given (in the opinion of the worshippers) to the fleeting as well as the permanent hopes and fears of erring, and rejoicing, and penitent, men and women, we shall be glad if they will use the same building with us, as a pledge of Christian brotherhood and an acknowledgment that, however far apart our courses may seem to lie, we steer by one compass and seek one port.

I take it that some at least amongst you may have detected a noteworthy gap in what I have been saying in this opening address. The prospectuses and pamphlets of the numerous corporations and individuals who are just now engaged in this work of settling and developing the unoccupied lands on this glorious con-

tinent are full of figures and statements show_ng the
rapidity with which enormous gain will be made in the
several regions to which they desire to attract settlers.
This being so, you may fairly ask, what have I, standing
here as the representative of the founders of this
settlement, to say upon this subject ?

I answer them broadly and frankly: we have nothing
to say.   We believe that our lands have been well
bought, and that those who settle here and buy from
us will get good value for their money, and will find it
as easy as it is at all well that it should be to make a
living here.   Beyond this we are not careful to travel.
Whether the lands will double or quadruple in value
before you have fairly learned how to live on them ;
whether you will make five, or twenty, or one hundred,
per cent on your investments, we offer no opinion.
You can judge for yourselves of the chances, if these
are your main aims.   Speaking for myself, however, I
must say that I look with distrust rather than with
hope on very rapid pecuniary returns.   I am old-
fashioned enough to prefer slow and steady growth.   I
like to give the cream plenty of time to rise before you
skim it.

> The wise men wait ; it is the foolish haste,
> And, ere the scenes are in the slides would play,
> And while the instruments are tuning, dance.

So far as I have been able to judge, these new settlements are being, as a rule, dwarfed and demoralised by
hurrying forward in the pursuit of gain, allowing this
to become the absorbing propensity of each infant community.   Then follows, as surely as night follows day,
that feverish activity of mercantile speculation which is

the great danger and, to my mind, the great disgrace of our time.   If it must come it must, but, so far as we are concerned, it shall get no help or furtherance here.

On the other hand, all that helps to make healthy, brave, modest, and true men and women will get from us all the cordial sympathy and help we are able to give.   In one word, our aim and hope are to plant on these highlands a community of gentlemen and ladies ; not that artificial class which goes by those grand names, both in Europe and here, the joint product of feudalism and wealth, but a society in which the humblest members, who live (as we hope most if not all of them will to some extent) by the labour of their own hands, will be of such strain and culture that they will be able to meet princes in the gate, without embarrassment and without self-assertion, should any such strange persons ever present themselves before the gate tower of Rugby in the New World.

CHAPTER II.

LATEST VIEWS.

(Reprinted from February Number of *Macmillan's Magazine.*)

So many persons have shown a desire to know more of this enterprise than can be gathered from the original prospectus, or the pamphlets which have followed it, that it may be well to give here some further account of what has been done hitherto, and what is contemplated.

First, as to the class of persons who may be advised to go to Rugby, Tennessee, with a view to settlement there. Every one not of independent means intending to make the experiment should ask himself seriously the question, "Am I prepared for some years, during the working hours of the day, to live the life of a peasant? or, in other words, to earn my living out of the soil by my own labour?" Unless he can answer, and answer confidently, in the affirmative, he had better not go. If he can, he may go safely, as he will find there as great variety of occupations to choose from as in any part of the United States, or our colonies. Soil, climate, situation, all point to a varied industry. The settler may raise sheep, cattle, or hogs; he may grow any kind of fruit or vegetables, or (should he prefer to follow the lead of the few native

farmers of the district) corn, maize, and other cereals ;
he may devote himself to the culture of poultry, or
bees ; he may take to lumbering, and help to supply
the saw-mills with logs, or the merchants with staves
for casks.   One or more of these industries he will
have to learn to live by, unless indeed he chances to
be a good mechanic.   For carpenters, masons, and
brickmakers, who know their business, there is a good
opening at good wages ; but these are in demand
everywhere in new countries.

I have said that the settler will have to lead a
peasant's life during working hours ; and it is this
limitation, " during working hours," which forms one
of the chief attractions of the settlement.   For at
other times, when his work is done, he will find
himself in a cultivated society, within easy reach of all
the real essentials of civilisation, beginning with a
good library.   In short, whoever is ready " to put
himself into primary relations with the soil and nature,
and to take his part bravely with his own hands in
the manual labour of this world " (as Mr. Emerson
puts it in his counsels to young Americans, in *Man the
Reformer*), will find here as favourable conditions for
his very sensible experiment as he is likely to get in
any part of the world.

Assuming then our young Englishman ready to
accept these conditions, and to start in life, resolute to
prove that he can make his two hands keep his head,
and need be under obligations to no one for a meal or
a roof, how is he to get to the scene of his experiment,
and what should he take with him in the shape of
outfit ?

First, as to outfit.   The less of it he takes the

better. One of the first and most valuable lessons which his new life will teach him is, that nine-tenths of what he has been used to consider the necessaries of life are only lumber. A good chest, or even a big leather bag, ought to hold all his worldly goods for the time being. Two or three stout suits of clothes, and several pairs of strong boots and gaiters, with flannel shirts, and a good supply of underclothing (including a leather waistcoat for the few bitterly cold winter days) and socks, will be ample. Slop clothes of all kinds he can get in America as cheap as at home, and not much worse; but they won't wear, especially the boots. These latter, I take it, it will always answer his purpose to get from England, paying the very heavy duty.

If he is a sportsman he may take his shot gun and rifle, but these must not be new, or they will be liable to duty. If he has none of his own, he had better buy in the United States, where all kinds of sporting weapons are very good, and cheaper than the English would be after payment of duty. For a revolver he will have no more occasion than in England. In this part of Tennessee they are only silly and somewhat dangerous toys; and I am glad to say that the magistrates of this, and all the neighbouring counties, are fining severely when cases of wearing arms are brought before them.

As to a fishing-rod and tackle, I am doubtful what to advise. There are two most tempting-looking streams, with pools and stickles which vividly excite one's piscatorial nerves at first sight, and give reasonable hope that monsters of the deep must haunt there. But further acquaintance dispels the pleasant illusion. Whatever the cause may be—probably because there

has never been, a close-time in these streams since
the creation, and the natives are wasteful as well
as very keen sportsmen—a bass of three or four inches
long is the biggest fish to be heard of.

That some sensible understanding will soon be
established as to the fishing there is much reason to
hope ; but, as it will take some years in any case
before it can be worth while to throw a line there,
the young settler had better perhaps leave his angling
gear at home.

And the same may be said for tool chests, and
implements of all kinds. If a youngster has a favourite
set which he has been using in those excellent workshops which some of our public schools have at last
established, sentiment may be allowed to carry the
day, and he may find it worth while to take his proved
tools with him. Otherwise, he will avoid much
trouble and annoyance at the custom-house by going
without, and will get the articles when he wants them
quite as good and not much dearer, at Cincinnati.

His chest or bag will of course find a corner for
some photographs and other home memorials, and
possibly for a favourite book or two. But of these
latter he may be saving, as he will find a good free
library already on the spot.

The great thing is to remember in all his prepara-
tions that he is going to try an experiment, which
may not succeed. If it should, he can easily run home
in a year or two for his " lares and penates." If not,
it will be very much better for him not to have to
bring them away. This would look like defeat, while
no such inference could fairly be drawn from the
packing up of one box, and the distribution amongst

those whom he leaves behind him in the settlement of whatever will not fit into it.

But he must have some money also ? Yes, but very little will serve his turn ; in fact I had almost said the less the better. If he is at all in earnest about what he is doing, a week or two will be enough to turn round in, see the place and the neighbourhood, settle what he is best fitted for, and make arrangements to begin working at that particular business. If for that week he even takes a room at the hotel, and lives there—the most costly course open to him—it will only cost him some £2. For a much smaller sum he can be put up at one of the boarding-houses. At the end of that time he ought to be able at least to earn enough to keep himself.[1] He will, if he is wise, at once become a shareholder in the town commissary (or supply association), which will cost him $5 or £1 ; and he may also like to join the club (which controls the lawn-tennis ground and the musical gatherings, and otherwise caters for the social life of the settlement), and to support the vestry or the choir. But we may take £5 as the maximum sum which it will need to make him free of all the nascent institutions of the infant settlement ; and if he can command another £10 to tide him over a week or two's failure of employment or health, he will have quite as much of the mammon of unrighteousness as is at all likely to be good for him at starting.

I am speaking now only of young men not yet of age, who seem likely to be the great majority of the

---

[1] The experience of the last few months has proved that young men going out without previous training cannot earn enough to support themselves at once. They should arrange to board for a year at least with one of the farmers, which they can do for £60.

settlers at present. For older men no longer under disability, who control their own funds and may be supposed to know their own minds, of course the case is different. Command of capital may make a great difference to them in their start, as many openings are occurring of which a man with funds under his immediate control will be able to avail himself. And even for younger men, where they or their friends can afford such an outlay, it will probably be desirable to make some arrangement with one of the present settlers, by which board and instruction may be obtained at a very reasonable cost, with the prospect possibly of a partnership in future. I only wish to say that, so far as I can judge, any young man who can command such an outfit and sum as I have named, in addition to his journey money, and goes out with a resolute determination to get on by hard work, may start for Rugby with good prospects of making an independence under pleasant and wholesome conditions of life.

The cost of getting out will depend in some measure on whether the emigrant is able, or desirous, to avail himself of the arrangements made by the Board. If he can do this, he may get to Sedgemoor, the Rugby station on the Cincinnati Southern Railway, for fifteen guineas, first-class; £12 : 10s. intermediate, and £8 : 10s. steerage. This route is by Philadelphia, and the train for Cincinnati is in waiting alongside the pier, where the steamers of the American line land their passengers. If he prefers, or is obliged, to go by New York, his sea-voyage will be at the ordinary fares ; but the agent of the Board at New York will furnish him with tickets to Sedgemoor at a reduced charge.

Going as fast as he can, he has thirty-six hours' railway after landing to get to Sedgemoor. As, however, he will probably like, at any rate, to sleep at Cincinnati on his road (even if he should be able sternly to waive aside the attractions of the eastern cities), we may look for him there some three days after his arrival in America.

Sedgemoor is a small clearing in the middle of the forest, through which the railway has been running for the last thirty miles. He is already some 1200 feet above the sea level, as he has been creeping up by gentle inclines ever since he entered the forest country. From this point the line descends again gradually to the South, till it reaches the Tennessee river and its terminus at Chatanooga. But when he is landed at Sedgemoor he is still some 600 feet below the level of Rugby, and he commences the ascent at once. There is a broad road, graded right away from the station to the town for six miles and upwards, through land belonging to the Board, and he begins the ascent within one hundred yards of the line. As soon as he is up this first ascent the road runs almost all the way along the ridge of a water-shed, to the Clear Fork river, upon the further bank of which the town of Rugby lies. The drive should be instructive to him, not mainly for the charm of the scenery, or the glimpses he will get here and there of the distant blue mountains of North Carolina away to the east, but for the specimen it will give him of the sort of work he will soon be employed on. Most likely his first job will be to clear similar land at so many dollars an acre, either for the Board or some of the settlers. The whole of the ridge on either side this road is specially

I

adapted for fruit-growing; so the farms are laid out in
forty or fifty acres, with only a small frontage to the
road.   Settlers who wish to start in fruit and vegetable
culture, can buy larger tracts to the rear at smaller
prices, if they wish to secure a larger area for
future use.

A year hence, it is hoped that, on crossing the Clear
Fork Bridge, the visitor will find himself opposite to a
public building which will serve as a gate-house to the
town, and where a register will be kept of all the inhabitants for the convenience of strangers; but as the
gate-house at present only exists on paper, he will have
to go to the office of the Board, some three-quarters of
a mile further on, in the centre of the town of the
future, for any information he may need.   On the
way he will pass the church, fronting the main avenue
along which his way lies, and will see the commissary
and the boarding-houses lying back on what will be
important side streets.   A number of private houses
in different stages of buildings—few, I fear, finished
as yet, the supply of building materials being sadly
behind the demand—line the main avenue, till it
terminates in a sweep which will bring him to the
Tabard, the hotel, which stands almost on the highest
point at the west end of the town, within a couple of
hundred yards or so of the thickly-wooded gully, some
two hundred feet deep, through which the second
stream, the White Oak, runs to its junction with the
Clear Fork half a mile away.   At the Tabard, if not
at the office, he will find the manager and other
officials of the Board, and will obtain all such advice
and assistance as he may need, both with respect to
his immediate housing, and to his future plans.

It may be well to refer shortly, in conclusion, to
several points on which a good deal of misunderstanding seems still to exist.

And first as to the commissary, to which reference
has been already made.   Doubts seem still to haunt
some minds as to the intentions of the Board in respect of the freedom of trade at Rugby.   We can best
answer, perhaps, by repeating what was said in the
address delivered by the representative of the Board
on the 5th of October 1880, which contains the truth,
the whole truth, and nothing but the truth :—

"We have all of us a number of imperative wants which
must be provided for and satisfied day by day.   We want food,
clothes, furniture, and a great variety of things besides, which
our nurture and culture have made all but essential to us.
These must all be provided here, either by each of us for himself or by some common machinery.   Well, we believe that it
can be done best by a common machinery, in which we should
like to see every one take a hand.   We have a 'commissary'
already established, and have used that word rather than 'store'
to indicate our own wishes and intentions, as a commissary is
especially a public institution.   Our wish is to make this commissary a centre of supply, and that every settler, or at any rate
every householder here, should become a member and part-
owner of it.   The machinery by which this can be done is
perfectly familiar in England and here also.   If it is adopted,
the cost price of establishing the present commissary, as it
stands, will be divided into small shares of five dollars each, so
that the poorest settler may not be inconvenienced by the outlay for membership.   Every one will get whatever profits are
made on his own consumption, and the business will be directed
and superintended by a board of council chosen by the members
themselves.   In this way again we shall have a common interest and common property, and in the supplying of our own
daily wants shall feel that, if one member suffers, all suffer ; if
one rejoices, all rejoice.   In this way, too, if we please, we may
be rid once for all of the evils which have turned retail trade

into a keen and anxious, and, generally, a dishonest scramble in older communities ; rid of adulteration, of false pretences, of indebtedness, of bankruptcy. Trade has been a potent civiliser of mankind, but only so far and so long as it has been kept in its place as a servant. As a master and an idol it has proved a destroyer in the past like all other idolatries, and its proving itself so in the present in many places we know of. Let us, as a community, take hold of it and master it here from the first, and never release our grasp and control of it."

This commissary has now been worked for three months by the settlers with excellent results. So far as I know, every one of them belongs to it, and the supplies of all kinds are satisfactory. But no one need belong unless he pleases, and there is nothing to hinder him from supplying himself elsewhere, or from setting up a store on his own account if so minded. The only restriction is on the sale of liquor, which is strictly prohibited. If he will have it he must import it for himself, and keep it to himself.

Again, it is equally untrue that any exclusive arrangement is contemplated as to church affairs. It is true that there is only one church, and that at present the only church organisation is under the Bishop of Tennessee, who has appointed two lay readers, who are responsible for the church services. But it has been specially stipulated that the building is open to the use of settlers of any denomination of Christians who wish to use it, and it is hoped that this arrangement may work satisfactorily in the future, as it has hitherto.

There only remains, I think, one point upon which anything need be said. It has been asked why such a settlement should not rather have been taken to an English colony, or to one of the Western States ; and the founders have been accused of a want of patriotism in the one case, and want of foresight in the other, for having selected a Southern State of the Union for their experiment.

As to our colonies, the distance from home is the answer as to all of them except Canada. From Rugby, if a settler is wanted at home he can be there within two weeks instead of six. As to Canada proper, the long winter and the difficulty of finding openings for varied industries on one spot, would have turned the scale in any case. And the same may be said of the North-western States of the Union. The prairie lands of Iowa, Kansas, and other States, above all of the Canadian province of Manitoba, are far richer ; but droughts, flies, difficulties of drainage, and from five to six months' enforced idleness, so far as agriculture is concerned, had to be considered.

And as to the question of patriotism, speaking now for myself alone, I must say it seems to me that the most patriotic thing an Englishman can do just now is to help in drawing as close as possible the bonds which unite his country to the United States. Unhappily, as I think, the imperial or anti-Continental policy (as I believe it is called) in Canada is not working in this direction. The determination of both political parties in the Dominion to construct at an enormous cost the long section of the Canada Pacific Railway, to the north of Lake Superior, seems to contemplate the possibility in the future of hostilities between the two countries. An Englishman's first wish should be to make this impossible, and I do not know how he can do this better than by sending all that can be spared of our best blood into the United States.

The objection to this policy here takes many shapes,

but is really founded on jealousy of the growing power
and prosperity of the English-speaking Republic, and
a fear lest its people should outstrip England in other
ways as decisively as they have already done in the
extent of their home territory.   Such jealousy may be
allowed to be natural, but is neither wise nor dignified.
We do not admire a father wincing at the success of
a son, who has built up for himself a bigger business
than that of the old firm, or has acquired more acres
than are numbered in the paternal estate.   Why
should we regard as patriotic in a nation what is
only contemptible in an individual ?

And again, speaking for myself only, I am free to
admit that the resolve arrived at, without reference to
any but economical considerations, to make the experiment in a Southern State was, to me, particularly welcome.
What we English want, looking to the future, is, not
only that England and America should be fast friends,
but that the feeling of union in the States themselves
should be developed as soundly and rapidly as possible
—that all wounds should be healed, and all breaches
closed, finally and for ever—for the sake of our race
and of mankind.   Much still remains to be done for
this end, and I am convinced that a good stream of
Englishmen into the Southern States may and will
materially help on the good cause.

No Englishman, according to his powers and opportunities, worked harder than I by tongue and pen
twenty years ago, against the cause for which the
Southern States staked all that was dearest to them in
their struggle to break up the nation and perpetuate
slavery.   I held then, and hold still, more strongly than
ever, that they were in the wrong, and that their suc-

cess would have been the greatest misfortune the world could have suffered in our time. But I am glad now, by lending such small help as I can in building up some of their waste places, to show my respect and good will for a people of English blood, who fought through one of the gallantest fights of all history, against overwhelming odds, though for a bad cause.

CHAPTER III.

AN ADDRESS

DELIVERED IN BIG SCHOOL, RUGBY, AT THE REQUEST OF
DR. JEX BLAKE.—*April 7th,* 1881.

I AM here to-day in obedience to a summons from the
head-master——embodying a wish, it would seem, of
several of his colleagues, as well as of a large number of
boys——to give explanations and answer questions concerning a new settlement in the United States, founded
in the autumn of last year by a corporation of Englishmen and Americans, known as the Board of Aid to Land
Ownership, and called Rugby.   The points upon which
I understand you specially to wish for information are,
first, why we have chosen this name; what meaning
we attach to it; what we intend it to signify? and,
secondly, what sort of a place it is; what sort of people
are there; and what are their intentions and prospects?

Let me at once acknowledge the right, not only of
your head-master, but of the youngest boy in this
school, to ask such questions.   You are all of you the
inheritors of an honoured name and of famous traditions, for which you do well to be jealous.   The head-
master is only the chief trustee for the time being of
the name and the traditions of this place, of which the
youngest boy sitting on those topmost benches should
also feel himself, in his own place, to be as truly a

trustee as the head-master.   You are all, I am sure, resolved that the name of Rugby, and the traditions
associated with that name, shall take no harm so far
as you are concerned.   And I trust that they are
equally precious to me, who have at any rate an older
claim to the name of Rugbeian than any one now
actively connected with this school.   There is no one
who owes more than I to Rugby, and no one who in
return is more jealous of the honour of the name, or
desires more earnestly that no harm or stain may
come to it through his agency in any part of the
world.

And so I very willingly address myself to this
task, and hope to satisfy you on all the points you
have raised.   In answering the first of your questions,
however, I shall have to tell a somewhat long story,
and to touch on subjects which probably my younger
hearers from the 4th form downwards will not think
much to the point, and will be somewhat bored by.
I can only ask for a little of their patience, on the
undertaking that I will come round as soon as I can to
what they want specially to hear about.

Having a long road to travel then, the sooner I
start on it the better.   It is all but forty years since I
left this school, after having been here as a boy for
eight years.   That, as the boy who hates mathematics
most amongst my lower school hearers will no doubt
readily admit, brings up my connection with Rugby to
very nearly half a century ; and this half century has
been probably the most momentous or revolutionary in
all our English history.   I mean that our England
of to-day is more changed from the England of fifty
years since—externally and internally, in her relation

to the visible and invisible worlds—than any previous England ever changed in the like time.   Take one fact in illustration of this.   There was no railway from London to Birmingham when I came to school here. It was indeed begun and running for some twenty miles out of London; but in my first half year I remember well going to see the first sod turned for the line of the London and Birmingham Railway down in the fields between the town and the Avon.   Almost directly afterwards came the agitation for free trade; and, by the time I took my degree at Oxford, the whole of England was covered with railways, and all her ports were thrown open to the world's commerce.

This is but a sample of the noiseless and bloodless revolution which has been going on at increasing speed ever since those days.   Men have done more in this half century towards the conquest of the material world than in many previous centuries.   They have made steam their beast of burthen, and the lightning their message-bearer; and, having become experts in the art of exploring the secrets of nature, and using them for practical purposes, are evidently on the eve of still greater discoveries and triumphs.   And nature, as usual, has been a liberal mistress, and has poured her rewards with full hands on those who have read her laws aright, and so discovered her secrets.   A flood of wealth has been poured on England in this time, such as probably never came before to any nation; and her material prosperity has increased by leaps and bounds.

There is nothing which tries individual character so shrewdly as wealth coming suddenly and in plethoric abundance; and what is true of individuals is true of

nations.   Without going all lengths with those who
maintain that sudden wealth must necessarily lower
and degrade the character, I am bound to confess
that in our case it has had a subtle and not a healthy
influence on our aims and standards of life, as well
as on our habits.   In the intoxication of this great
materialist movement we English have somewhat lost
our heads — have come to an alarming extent to
acknowledge the heaping up of wealth to be the true
end of all effort ; and the hero, the man most worthy
of admiration, the happy man, he who has succeeded
best in this business.   The desire and respect for
wealth has always, of course, been strong enough ; but
up to our time it has been decently draped and
cloaked : now the idol stands out, naked and not
ashamed, and absorbing a large share of the genuine
worship of our people.

Happily, however, this, which (for want of a better
name) I have called the materialist movement of our
time has not had the field to itself.   Side by side
with, and opposing it foot to foot, has grown up
another great movement, which (again for want of a
better term) I will call the educational movement.
This has been constantly appealing to the higher
instincts and faiths of the nation, as the other to its
lower appetites and greeds—maintaining a protest for
the invisible against the visible.   The essence of that
protest has been, that the aim of man's life is not to
heap up wealth, but to bring body and intellect into
perfect obedience to the will, and the will into perfect obedience to the conscience.   It has proclaimed
that no command of material things, no success in
piling them up, can compensate for the want of self-

control—that "he that ruleth himself" is still as in the
time of the son of Sirach "greater than he that taketh
a city"—and that it is not the millionaire, the most
skilful and successful collector of what may be tasted
and touched, who should be the object of our admiration and imitation, but rather, in the words of Sir H.
Wolton (which no doubt are familiar to many here,
who must have had to turn them into longs and shorts),
the man who

> ———" is free from servile bands,
> Of hope to rise, or fear to fall,
> Lord of himself, tho' not of lands,
> And having nothing yet hath all."

Now the stronghold of this educational movement
has been our public schools, and the first and great
apostle of it was Dr. Arnold, the man who has given
a world-wide fame to this place.   His name, and
that of Rugby, are as much identified with the educational movement in the England of our day, as that of
Luther and Wittenberg are with the religious movement
of the fifteenth century.   Its strength is shown by
the extraordinary increase in numbers of our public
schools, which have grown from seven or eight to
upwards of forty if we take the most conventional
standard, and to about three hundred if we judge our
schools by the only true test, their aims and their
methods.

And from these many centres an influence has
been going out, and is becoming stronger year by
year which more than any other has helped to arrest
the materialism of our time so far as it has been
arrested at all.   A far larger proportion of the generation of Englishmen now coming to the front are

affected by the public school spirit than ever before ;
and, as a natural result, the characteristics of that
spirit will be felt more and more in all departments of
our national life.   Let me name the most salient of
those characteristics,—reticence, hardiness, independence, a high sense of honour, especially in all money
matters, and good fellowship, manifesting itself in
readiness to stand by and help one another.   The
mere naming of them is enough to bring home to us
their worth as antidotes to materialism and Mammon
worship.   In a blatant and luxurious age, what more
valuable than the sort of reticence and hardiness which
becomes a second nature at such schools as this ?   In
my time here there was a sort of proverb current,
comprising the whole duty of boys as it was then
understood, " Fight fair, fall light, and hold your
tongue."   This may perhaps be a somewhat barbarous
and obsolete formula to-day, so let us take a better
expression of the same idea from one of Mr. Lowell's
later poems (which I heartily commend to the upper
school as about the best reading of that kind I know).

> " Yes, I think I do see, after all's said and sung,
>   Take this one rule of life, and you never will rue it ;
> 'Tis just—do your own duty, and hold your own tongue,
>   And each man were royal himself, if he knew it."

In an age when our prophets (like Mr. Carlyle) are
telling us that the modern Englishman's hell is the
fear of not making money, what more valuable than
scrupulousness even to Quixotism in every transaction
involving a shilling ?   In an age which has been
taught that unrestricted competition is the true rule of
life, and cash payment the sole nexus between man and
man, what more valuable than the sort of tie which

binds men bred at the same public school together all over the world,

But stop ! Is this all true ? Are you not drawing on your imagination, or on memories of a time which has long gone by, for your characteristics of the public school spirit ? I am quite prepared to be pulled up in this way, and to be told that English boys are no longer reticent ; but as blatant, as fond of making their sweet voices heard over any petty grievance, real or fancied, as any other section of a blatant nation—no longer hardy ; but bent on feeding copiously, and lying soft—no longer independent ; but full of an idea that it is some one's duty to provide for them, that by rights they ought to be, like the sacred bulls of the Brahmins, able to go about anywhere, eating and drinking whatever they like, and lying down wherever they like, at the expense of the community—no longer scrupulous about money, but greedy for being pouched, tipped, for getting money at all events. And I am free to admit that there is much in the popular literature of the day—something even in the frequency and persistency with which (as their published sermons show) your own head-master, and many another, make a point of enforcing the duty of plain living and high thinking. And no doubt the materialist influence, which, as I have said, has been so all but dominant in England for the last half century, must to some extent have penetrated our schools, and left its baleful trail in their courts. No doubt, in many individual instances, where home influences are too strong—perhaps in some schools, if any there be, in which governing bodies and staff are not doing their duty, and setting good examples in their own lives—the characteristics I have assumed to be of the essence of the public school spirit, may not now be found.   Nevertheless, as a broad fact, I maintain that these are, here and now, in this year 1881, still its characteristics, and I found my opinion not only upon the boys of my own kin, but upon good opportunities of intimate acquaintance with several of our large schools.   And I believe that this spirit is prevailing more and more in England, and will prevail yet more and more in the future, and I look forward very hopefully to the work which it will accomplish for this nation.

Meantime, however, there is one notable result of its progress ; and that is, the vast surplus over home-needs of boys and young men full of this public school spirit.   There are already very many more than can possibly find suitable work at home ; and, if their training has gone more than skin deep, they will not brook a listless half occupied life, or to feel themselves a burthen on their families.   Moreover their families are likely for the next few years, at anyrate, to be much poorer than they have been, and in no condition or temper to keep strapping young fellows in the full vigour of health and strength, at home in idleness.

What then are they to do with themselves ?   What advice can we older folks give them ?   I have no hesitation myself in saying, " Go back to the land, and take with you the spirit and traditions of this public school training you have had at home."   There is no other career in which each of you will find himself so thoroughly master of his own life, free to build it up after his own ideal——none in which the characteristics of his training——hardiness, reticence, independence, scrupulousness in money matters, will stand him in better stead, or have so free a field for development.

And so now I have brought you round at last, and I think even my young friends up there on the back benches will see why a forest settlement in Tennessee is called Rugby.   It is hoped that it will prove to be a place specially suited to men trained as you are being trained here; and that the spirit which such men carry with them will lose none of its strength by exportation, but will prevail and keep the life of a new society, fresh and strong in that new land.

So now I can turn to the inquiries, What is the place like ? ˙ What sort of life do they lead out there ?   In each case I will call more competent witnesses than myself as to what Rugby is like.   Here is a letter from a very distinguished Etonian and Cambridge man, now settled there, who has taken mining engineering as a profession.

29th October 1880.

My connection with the enterprise dates from December 1879, when the Board asked me to come out and make a geological survey of their present and future possessions round here.   I was out all January and February, then went home for three months, and came out again in June ; and find myself getting anchored faster every day, as life here is a pleasing mixture of all the delights and none of the discomforts of the backwoods.

I am the only Etonian now on the spot.   H—— of Ainger's house was here in August, but has gone home ; and P—— of Dupin's was here on a flying trip the other day—he is settling one of his brothers in Iowa, and I hope went away convinced of his mistake in not sending him here.   Send us out *quam primum* a fresh supply of the hardy tug and untamed oppidan, that Alma Mater may rule the roast.   There is no great assemblage of public schoolmen here at present—one each of Rugby, Wellington, Malvern, and Brighton, will about fill the bill ; but other specimens are expected before long, and the sooner the better.

Stock farming will, I think, be the principal thing to take to, —for the present at any rate. As time goes on, and more land is cleared of timber, corn and other crops will increase in import-ance, while fruit and garden " *sass* " will yield most abundantly, and pay anybody well who goes in for them. Apples have gone to waste in waggon-loads this year all round here for want of hands to pick them. One man offered me 200 bushels of splendid apples if I would come and fetch them away.

Timber is going to be a big thing. I am now making in-quiries as to the possibility of supplying the north country collieries from here, and hope to bring the British timber-merchant to a sense of his sins. Settling on these heavily timbered lands means hard work for the first few years : but seeing that your timber is worth many times the price you give for your land, and that you increase the value of your land many times more by clearing it, you evidently get a considerable *quid* for your *quo* in the shape of hard work.

All this mountain is coal land, and every ton will have to be got out some time or another, though the date cannot be given as yet. But seeing that here alone of the American continent—or of the world as far as I know—coal and red hematite lie cheek by jowl along a big fault, which throws carboniferous against lower silurian rocks, it is not difficult to infer blast furnaces at no distant date ; and the thing is improved by the recent discovery and partial development in the mountains east of here, of heavy beds of magnetic ore, which are said to show a higher percentage of metallic iron than any ore hitherto handled here or elsewhere.

Just round the town here there is no great development of coal, but building stone and fire and brick clay enough to build London, which is all as it should be, as it is to be feared that the Smoke Prevention Act would not work well in this section. But there is a very pretty water power on the two streams Clear Fork and White Oak, which meet here. We are moving to get the first to work for a water supply, which is urgently needed.

The present population of Rugby is about 120. The hotel has been running since the 5th inst., and has hardly had a bed vacant since that time. There is a " boarding-house," a " bar-racks," an " asylum," an office, and various shanties, and a " com-missary " or store, which has been put on a co-operative footing.

K

A library has been formed, and we have already got promises, private and official, of nearly 4000 volumes ! This necessitates a good building, for which we are sending round the hat. If it reaches you I hope the tile will depart heavier by a few coppers. As for the tennis club, whist, etc., and the rest, they are written in the books of Vacuus Viator, so you will see that we have what is known as a " bully time " on this continent.

If you know of any good fellows who are thinking of the States, I believe they can't do better than come here, for a look at the place at any rate.   Sheep is the thing, in the opinion of good judges at any rate, to begin with ; then mixed farming as the place gets cleared.

Then, in answer to the question what kind of life will have to be led there, I will read you the last letter received from a nephew of mine, aged twenty-one, a Marlburian, who with his younger brother, late a scholar of Westminster, aged nineteen, whose health broke down at school, is settled on a Texan ranche, a long way from Rugby no doubt, but with far less advantageous surroundings than settlers at Rugby will have :—

7th March 1881.
The success of Hal and myself is now assured, and we know it.   The first spring I was here was the drought, when nobody raised anything, which was discouraging.   Last year we did fairly for our first year of farming and sheep, but this year finds us well ahead of our business.   Our sheep could not be doing better.   Last year's experience in the lambing season taught us what was necessary to have for the proper management of the lambs, and our system of lambing-pens and pasturing is superb. The lambs are dropping like hail (eight to-day), and they are at once drafted off into the pasture, where they remain for a few days till the ewes " take " properly to them.   Each lamb is marked with a red spot or line on a part of its body, and the ewe is marked in the same way on the same part of its body, so that we know exactly which lamb belongs to which ewe ; and a record is kept of the date the lamb is born, and of its mark, so as to know when it can with safety be allowed to run with the

flock. When a few days old, and the ewe has taken properly to the lamb, they are turned into the field where the oats are coming up splendidly. This brings a flush of milk on the ewe, and gives the lamb a good start. The last lamb born to-day made our fiftieth lamb. We have had several weeks of the most glorious weather ; in our shirt sleeves from morning to night, and yet not too hot to work all through the day, and we have had a tremendous lot of work lately. We have about four acres of oats growing well, and two days ago I put in about an acre of corn ; and to-day I hauled up the "camp tricks" to the tent at the Schulz field, as I am going to camp up there and plough up for corn. Our spring onions are coming up splendidly, and this morning I put in our seed sweet potatoes, from which grow the vines which are planted out later on. The vines produce the potatoes, so to speak. I have a seed-bed with beets, cabbages, lettuces, squashes, and cauliflowers in, and some of them are beginning to come up ; and I have a bed of very early corn in, and I expect we shall be the first round here to have roasting ears ; and my ground for beans, melons, and tomatoes, etc., is all ploughed and ready to be planted as soon as spring has regularly set in—at least as soon as all chance of cold has gone, for spring has set in some time ; the grass is growing up green, and the wild flowers and bushes are all opening, and the nights are getting quite warm. We planted out sixteen fruit trees—apples and peaches, and they are all doing well ; and the comfreys have been green for weeks, and we are planting out a large patch of them this spring ; you have no idea how useful they are in case of a sick ewe. I forget whether I told you that the grass seeds did not come to anything, but that the clover is all coming up and looking well. I think it is going to prove a very valuable addition to the herbage here. We planted it on about half an acre in the pasture, and have fenced off a little patch to keep the sheep and calves off, and let it run to seed. We are still getting plenty of milk from old "Gentle," and within a few weeks we shall have more milk than we shall know what to do with, unless we get a pig, as we have several good cows going to calve. The English ewes begin to lamb the day after to-morrow, and Flora, the collie that Mr. Hewett sent me, pups to-morrow ; and we have two hens hard at work sitting, and the whole "boiling" of them are cackling and laying, so we are increasing to a great extent. And lastly, I forgot old Molly the mare.

She has gone off to her old range preparatory to having a colt ;
and another mare of ours who runs between here and Boerne is
also going to have a colt.   Oh ! and then the cat ; she's going
to have kittens.   I think I've told you about everything now.
We have all had a fit of letter-writing to-night.   At this time of
year I fear we neglect it a good deal.   From daylight to late at
night we are kept agoing I assure you.   First it's cooking
breakfast, and milking, and separating newly-born lambs and
their ewes from the flock, then turning out the flock and draft-
ing the older lambs and ewes into the field, and holding refract-
ory ewes for the lambs to suck.   Then there's ploughing or
planting all day ; then the flock comes in, and more new lambs
to fix, and more suckling and feeding ; then supper to cook and
washing-up to do ; and by the time one has finished supper one
feels as though one could fall asleep at the table.   It's glorious
fun though, and we enjoy the life immensely.   I have to shave
now ; it is my Sunday morning's job.   Hal is just off (11 P.M.)
to his tent up by the sheep-pen, where he has his cot and sleeps
every night now.   You have no idea how well he is looking ;
you would hardly know him.

You will have gathered from the latter that they are
settlers of two years' standing, and, I may add, that they
have had about £700 of capital between them.

You may take this, then, as a fair sample of the sort
of life which settlers at Rugby will have to lead, at
any rate for several years.   It means hard and constant manual labour at one or another kind of farming
operations.   Unless a young man is prepared for this
he had better not go.   Does it cross your minds that
if this be so your present education is a mistake ; and
a very bad preparation for the life to which many of
you will have to turn in the future ?   That is natural
enough, but an error.   Depend upon it, the higher
culture of all kinds you can get now, the happier and
better backwoodsmen you will be, if that should prove
to be your destiny.   And let me remind you that the

worth of manual labour, as a part of the highest education, is getting to be more and more openly recognised
by the most successful and laborious men in all ranks.
Mr. Gladstone, for instance, has again and again advocated its claims, and bears practical testimony to the sincerity of his belief in his own method of taking relaxation.
The late Mr. Brassey invariably gave the advice—" above
all, teach him some handicraft thoroughly," to the crowds
of people who used to consult him about their sons.
One of the most rising of the junior members of the
present Government goes straight to digging in his
garden whenever he gets a holiday.   Besides, is the
truth not admitted now in this, and I believe almost
all the other public schools, by the establishment of
workshops, in which carpentering, turning, and other
handicrafts are taught ?   I only wish it had been so in
my day, for I have felt the want of such training all
my life.   In my last year at school I was head of big
side, both of cricket and football ; and if the boys who
fill those onerous and responsible posts happen to be
present, they will bear me out, that he who holds them
has very limited time to give to inferior industries, such,
for instance, as the cultivation of Greek Iambics or Latin
Alcaics.   And, looking back over much that one has to
regret in the shape of misspent time, I am not at all
sure that I repent the hours taken from Greek and
Latin verses and given to organising big side matches
and playing them.   But of this I am quite sure, that I
should have been a better and happier, as well as a
handier, man all my life, if I had been able to give a
good portion of those hours to such work as you have
all of you the chance of learning on the other side of
the school close.

" But is there nothing more than this ?   Surely we have heard of lawn tennis, and bathing, and shooting parties coming home carrying deer on poles through the forest ? "   Yes, you have heard such stories no doubt—more than enough of them most likely.   Writers who have never been near the place and know nothing of the circumstances, have been funny and severe on the fact that the first settlers made a tennis ground before they began clearing, or digging, or ploughing.   They did so, in fact, because they had nothing else to do.   The titles were not perfected, so we couldn't sell them land, and they couldn't work on it.   And I doubt if they could have done a more sensible thing.   In the same way they did bathe a good deal, in a famous pool, ten feet deep, lying in the rhododendron bushes just below the town site ; and every now and then went out shooting and brought back a deer.   There will always be slack times in the busiest lives, when such pastimes are excellent, and I should advise every settler to take a good shot gun and rifle with him, and fishing-rod too, for before long we hope to have fine bass and other fish in our two fine streams. But these will only be the fringe of the life ; the staple of it will be hard continuous work, for some years at anyrate, till farms are cleared, fruit trees bearing, and flocks and herds have multiplied.   Those who prefer other ways of passing any leisure time they may have on their hands will find a famous library on the spot, contributed by the publishers, and various public societies, in America.

I don't know that there is anything more that I need say, and I have already outrun my time.   I would only beg you all, in conclusion, to remember that I am not here to preach an exodus to any of you boys who can see your way to an honest living by honest work at home here in England. That is the best life for yourselves and for your country. But for those who find after leaving school that they have no such outlook in England, I undoubtedly believe that they can't do better than go back to the land; and that they will not easily find a brighter or more hopeful place in which to try such an experiment than Rugby, Tennessee; while the name of their new home will keep up not only a sense of continuity in their lives, but the memory of this old world Rugby, to which, as the years go on, they will feel an ever-growing debt of affection and gratitude.

CHAPTER IV.

THE following report has been prepared by the Minister of Agriculture for the State of Tennessee :—

The Soil.

It is not claimed that the soil of Rugby, or the Cumberland plateau, is rich. On the contrary, it is generally poor, or at most only of medium quality. It is a rare thing in the United States to find rich soil, plenty of timber, perfect healthfulness and desirableness of climate, cheap land, convenient markets, and easy access to means of transportation, all combined. That Rugby possesses all these essentials to a happy home, except rich soil, no one, it is believed, will deny. It is equally true that the soil, by proper culture and handling, can be improved and made to yield remunerative crops.

The soil may be divided into five classes:—

1. Thin sandy soil, resting upon sandstone, which comes near the surface. This is unfruitful, both from original poverty of constitution and from a want of depth. Fortunately it does not occupy a large area, but is confined for the most part to the high lands adjoining streams. Timber scrubby.

2. Sandy soil, light, but deep. Upon this the most

succulent and nutritious grasses grow, and furnish a large amount of excellent pasturage. The prevailing timber is chestnut, oak, and pine.

3. Sandy soil, incumbent upon a mulatto clay. This, by reason of its clayey foundation, which enables it to catch and preserve fertilising material, is the best of all the upland soils of the mountain, and covers by far the largest area, especially on the lands belonging to the Rugby colony. It is naturally fertile upon the north hill-sides, having in such places a black colour, resembling the black prairie lands of Illinois. The black soil however is very limited. The general characteristics of this class of soil is a light grayish or yellowish colour, with a mulatto subsoil. The latter is very retentive, and holds all fertilisers applied. Extensive white oak forests occur upon it. Where there is a modification of this soil by the presence of small angular gravel the timber varies, and red oak, black oak, hickory, and pine, are associated with the white oak. Grape vines grow abundantly upon such soils.

4. The alluvium along the water courses, which is black in colour, friable and productive. The amount of this soil is inconsiderable.

5. Glebe lands—the beds probably of old marshes, in which has accumulated a large mass of vegetable débris. The soil of this is sometimes black, more often ashen in colour, and always charged with humic acid to such a degree as to be unproductive, unless thoroughly drained and sweetened by æration. No timber will flourish in such places except swamp maple, sweet gum, and other kinds adapted to wet lands.

The most important, because the most abundant in quantity, is the third class mentioned. Though comparatively thin and infertile, nothing is risked in saying that, in original strength and productiveness, it is far superior to any soils found in New England outside the valleys, and not one-half the expense need be incurred in bringing it to a higher degree of fertility, for three reasons :—

1*st*, The subsoil is not so porous as the subsoil in New England, where the drifted pebbles commingled with sand lie beneath all the soils on the elevated lands.

2*d*, This soil under consideration will, on account of the climate, grow a much larger number of green crops, which can be utilised in adding humus.

3*d*, Both the soil of New England and the soil of the plateau need the application of lime, and this article can be burned and applied for one-third the cost to the lands of the plateau that it can be applied to the soils of New England :—1st, because lime-rack is abundant and cheap, and is found in many valleys belonging to and contiguous to the lands of the company ; and 2d, because fuel—both coal and wood, exists in such quantities as to be practically without cost.

The land can further be improved by sowing the cowpea and turning under the vines. The climate and soil are both adapted to the growth of this legume, and, in the experience of the best planters south, no renovator—not even clover—is equal to the haulm of the pea. But clover also grows well on this soil. The writer has seen it growing at Greutli three feet high, upon a soil far more sandy and far less productive naturally, than upon the lands of the company. No fertiliser was applied to it except two bushels of plaster per acre, at a cost of less than $1 per acre.

Rye is another green crop that may be grown with success upon the silico-argillaceous soils of the plateau, also buckwheat, both of which are regarded as excellent crops for renovating the soil.

The most rapid improvement in the soil, however, can be obtained by the sowing of one or two crops of cowpeas during the year. One of these may be taken off for fodder and the other turned under. In this way the soil may be continually improved without the loss of a single crop. Nor is this mere surmise. It has been done again and again, not only on the plateau but on the sandy soils of West Tennessee. It may be laid down as a general rule that all lands which rest upon a clayey foundation can be rapidly improved by the application of manures, green or dry; and after manures have been applied for several years in succession, the land becomes a garden mould rich enough to produce any crop, and as easy to keep up thereafter as the most fertile virgin soil. The lands of the plateau have been kept in a condition of comparative infertility by the pernicious habit of annually burning the leaves, thus destroying the material for humus, and exposing the soil to the parching influence of the sun, drawing away all humidity, without which there can be no improvement in the productive capacity of any soil.

The Grasses which do well.

Herde grass (*Agnostis vulgaris*) and orchard grass (*Dactylis glimevata*) both grow well upon the mountain. The first, when occasionally top-dressed with stable manure, will yield grand crops for many years in succession. Clover, as has been mentioned, will also grow well by the application of a small quantity of sulphate of lime (plaster of Paris) in the spring. Esparsette or sanfoin (*Onobrychis sativa*) will suit the sandy soils of the plateau, and furnish an article of hay equal in every particular to the best clover hay. Gama grass would also be found to be a valuable accession to the forage crops of the plateau.

Crops.

It is not assumed that corn and wheat will do remarkably well, or be very profitable on the Cumberland plateau. The first requires rich alluvial soil for a heavy crop. In the natural state of the soil in this region, large yields of corn cannot be expected.

From twenty to twenty-five bushels per acre is as much as can be expected, and often it will fall below these figures. But by following the directions herein given for the improvement of the soil, after a few years a heavier yield may be expected. Corn is a great exhauster of the soil, and therefore the settlers should be exceedingly careful not to raise frequent crops of it on the same piece of land. This should be especially so until the land is brought up to a high degree of productiveness. The land should not be put in corn more than once in every five years. On such land a corn crop is not profitable. Raise as little as possible, and supply its place with other things.

Wheat.

Wheat will not make a remunerative crop upon the

virgin soil of the plateau, but experiments have demonstrated the fact that, by the application of two cords of manure to the acre, fifteen bushels may be raised.   The best course to pursue with this crop is to sow after a pea fallow ; and when the wheat crop is harvested the succeeding summer break the land and sow again in peas, the haulm of which will be ready to turn under in time to sow a crop of wheat the same autumn.   By continuing this practice from year to year, aiding the land with occasional dressings of manure, very good wheat crops may be produced on the same field for a succession of years.   The writer has known some very poor sandy soils to be brought to a high degree of fertility by pursuing this method. It is worthy of trial by the colonists.

Oats.

The remarks made above in reference to corn are also applicable to oats.   They exhaust the productive capacity of the soil very rapidly.   Therefore they should be sown on the same piece of land only at long intervals.   No wise farmer can afford to exhaust his soil in order to get a particular crop, especially a second crop, from his land.   To build up, and not to exhaust, is true wisdom.   He that does thus will get rich, while the opposite policy inevitably leads to poverty.

Rye.

The climate of Rugby is well suited to rye.   Wherever the soil is in good condition it will do well.   It requires good rich soil.   Rye makes a fine winter pasture.   When ploughed under in the spring, after it

gets a fair start in growth, it makes a fine fertiliser,
It can therefore be sown with profit for a fall and
winter pasturage, and also used for a fertiliser the next
spring or summer.

Sweet Potatoes.

Sweet potatoes do well on the sandy soil on the
plateau. They love a sandy loam, and require only a
moderately rich soil. If very rich they run too much
to vines and leaves. Stable manure well rotted, and
wood ashes, are excellent fertilisers for them. Where
the soil is suitable and the season good, the yield
should be from seventy-five to one hundred bushels
per acre. Further south, and in a lower latitude, the
yield per acre is much greater,—often reaching from
two to three hundred bushels.

For the ordinary purposes of sustaining life nothing
is cheaper or better. For cattle, horses, or hogs, they
have been proved by experiments to be equal to corn,
bushel for bushel. They contain quite as much nutri-
ment, and are more healthy. They are fed either raw,
or after they have been cooked.

At Rugby sweet potatoes can be made valuable for
marketing. They are a tropical production, and are
much sweeter grown in a warm climate. In Cincinnati and other northern cities they command high
prices, and especially the early ones. There is no
good reason why those cities should not draw their
main supply from the Cumberland plateau. As the
sweet potato loves a hot soil, it should be planted on
the south hill-sides or slopes. With good cultivation
one hundred and fifty bushels may be produced with
ease upon an acre of land.

Irish Potatoes.

The Irish potatoes raised on the high Cumberland lands are very superior, having an excellent flavour. They are greatly superior to those raised in the valleys of East or Middle Tennessee. They are also very productive on these lands. In them the farmers of Rugby have an unfailing source of income. All the cotton States draw their supplies of this universal article of food for winter consumption from the States north of them. Early potatoes can be raised in the southern States; but late ones for winter do not do well. Knoxville, Chatanooga, and Atalanta, will always be good markets for good winter potatoes. Hundreds of barrels raised in the north are sold every spring in Knoxville at good prices.

While there must ever remain a good market in the south for winter potatoes, Cincinnati will furnish a market for the early ones. They can be put into this market from Rugby several days—perhaps ten days, earlier than they can be from Ohio or Northern Kentucky. The very early ones command very high prices.

The soil suited for Irish potatoes is a rich loam. It cannot be too rich. They will do but little good on exhausted or very poor land. Well rotted stable manure, wood ashes, ground bone, hair, plaster, forest-leaves, are all good fertilisers for them. Wood ashes are perhaps the best of all.

Early potatoes should be planted in February if possible, and if the soil is suitably manured, 300 bushels per acre is not considered an exorbitant crop. Near Jersey city this number of bushels has been often gathered. A southern exposure is best if early

maturity is desired.   But for a late crop, the ground
should always be, when practicable, low-bottom or
north hill-sides.   Our fall seasons are generally dry
and hot, and therefore such ground should be chosen
as would be least affected by heat and drought.   The
early crop can be planted early in February, and the
late one the last of June or very early in July.   The
best varieties of early potato yet introduced are the
Early Rose and Snow Flake, and for the late crop the
Peachblow, Pink Eye, and Mountain Sprout.   Northern
grown seed, especially for the early crop, is decidedly
the best ; but if a second crop of early potatoes is
grown they make the best seed.   This can be done in
this climate by digging the first crop in June, exposing
them to the air for a few days, and then planting them
in land well prepared.   This practice is becoming very
common about Nashville.

Vegetables.

Nearly all vegetables will do well in the climate of
Rugby, where the soil is in good condition.   But
it must be borne in mind that all the vegetables,
like corn and Irish potatoes, require rich food.   It
is in vain to expect good returns without good care
and rich soil.

If gardening for the Cincinnati market should be
the object of any of the colonists, they had better
raise a general assortment, and not confine themselves
to a few articles, so that if one fails others may
succeed.   In gardening, it is never safe to rely upon
one or two articles.   Besides, if the gardener has to
attend market, he had better go with a full assortment
and supply.

There is one vegetable to which we invite especial attention, and that is—

Cabbage.

Perhaps no vegetable is so universally eaten, and largely consumed, in the United States, as cabbage. It forms a part of the daily food of nearly every family during the greatest part of the year. It is peculiarly the poor man's food. The reason is twofold; first, because most persons are fond of it; and second, because more food can be purchased of it for a small sum than of nearly anything else. It comes into use early in June, and continues in market until next spring, frequently until the next crop is ready for use. It is always in demand. It is easily kept through the winter. And in the south, in those localities where the soil and climate are suitable for its growth, no crop will pay better.

The settlers at Rugby must bear in mind that south of Tennessee it cannot be grown, except in high mountainous regions. Its habitat is a cold climate. Hence in the hot southern states it does no good. They must depend on the north for their fall and winter supply. Here, there is this wide region, from Wilmington to New Orleans, with all the interior to be supplied. The Cumberland plateau is the nearest region suitable for the growth of fine cabbage. Even at Knoxville, with a country north of it moderately well adapted to its growth, large quantities of it are brought from Virginia every winter and spring, and sold. No doubt this is true of Chattanooga and Nashville also.

The Cumberland lands and climate are admirably

L

suited for cabbage. Where the lands are made rich
with barn-yard manure, or with bone dust, phosphate,
or guano, all of which are admirable fertilisers for it,
it can be grown in great perfection. The writer saw
a head grown in the garden of Rugby, by Mr. Hill, on
poor, old land, which weighed, about the 6th October
last, before it was done growing, ten pounds.

Mr. Mosier, at Sunbright, has frequently raised
heads weighing from fifteen to twenty pounds, as the
writer is informed.

Early cabbage can no doubt be profitably raised for
the Cincinnati market. But it is late cabbage which
can be most profitably raised, for the Chattanooga,
Atalanta, and other southern markets.

That cabbage can be made a profitable crop at
Rugby, with the liberal use of fertilisers, is susceptible
of the clearest demonstration. If the plants are three
feet apart, 4840 can be grown on an acre. If two
and a half feet 6969 per acre. The latter distance is
sufficiently far apart if the crop is raised by hand.
The former is better, if a plough is used in cultivation.
Suppose the plants make heads which weigh, on an
average, five pounds, and that they will yield in
market a cent a pound. Then an acre planted two
and a half feet apart would produce $348·45 worth
of cabbage, and at three feet it would amount to
$242·00. If but half a cent a pound is realised, as
clear profit, the result would be in the one case
$174·22 and in the other $121·00 per acre. With
a good season, good culture, and with thorough fertilisa-
tion, there is every probability that the heads can be
made to average eight or ten pounds. The writer saw
cabbage selling in Knoxville at retail, by the small

dealers, January 4th 1881, at four cents a pound. The winter price is usually as much as two and a half cents a pound with the hucksters.   Of course the producer can get no such prices at wholesale.

No special skill is required to raise or take care of cabbage.   Aside from planting, it requires no more care or labour than corn.   It can be easily kept through the winter until spring.   The main point always to be kept in mind is, that it imperatively requires rich and well pulverised soil, or the liberal use of stimulating fertilisers.   Late cabbage should by all means be planted on low moist bottom lands, or on north hill-sides.   The ground cannot be made too rich for it.   Early cabbage should have a southern exposure.

The best varieties are, for early, Early Wyman, and Early Jersey Wakefield ; for late, Large Late Drumhead, and Large Flat Dutch.   Under all circumstances it is safe to assume that cabbage will yield as clear profit one half-cent a pound, and frequently much more.

Fruit Growing.

All the fruits of the temperate zone, possibly excepting peaches, as far as tested, do well on the tableland of Tennessee.

Apples.

Apples do remarkably well, and can be made a great success.   Those grown on this plateau have a fine flavour, fine colour, and are crisp and delicious. This has been clearly proved by the orchards of Mr. England and Dodge and Son, White County, Mr. Hill of Warren, and Mr. Caldwell of Franklin.   The latter bore away all the premiums for fine apples at the fairs in Nashville for several years in succession. His orchard occupied a position on the mountain, about 1900 feet above the sea. The fruit grown in these orchards has been pronounced equal to the best northern apples. The apple-trees on all the Cumberland lands are healthy and thrifty.

For this fruit there is a wide and ready market in southern cities. In the Cotton states, it must be remembered, that the apple is not much grown, and the fruit is quite inferior. Their winter supply is drawn nearly entirely from the north and north-west. Even in Knoxville, with a country surrounding it tolerably well adapted to the apple, especially on the high ridges, hundreds, perhaps thousands, of barrels of winter apples, are brought every year from New York, Michigan, Ohio, and other States, and sold at high prices. The same statement is no doubt true of Nashville, Chattanooga, and Atalanta.

Cincinnati will furnish a market for early apples, and the southern cities for winter marketing. For the reason that apples do best in a moderately cold climate, the ground selected for them should be as high as possible, and on the northern slopes, or on the tops of ridges. Besides this, the best soil is usually found on the north side of hills.

The following varieties have been tested in Tennessee, many of them on the Cumberland lands, and are known to suit this climate, and to be of excellent quality. Most of them, and possibly all, can be had at the nurseries of Ward and Brothers, London, Tennessee, or at Bird and Dew's, Knoxville. Both firms are reliable.

World's Wonder, Nickojack, Tennessee Red, Stinson, Golden Red, Fallawater, Volunteer or Peerie, Winesap, Golden Russett, Shockley, Grime's Golden, Berry Red, Striped Pairmain, Mountain Sprout, Pumpkin Limber Twigg, Early Strawberry, Early Harvest, Muskmellon, England's Seedling, Gravenstein, Peck's Pleasant, Northern Spry, Stine.

Do not purchase winter apple-trees in the north, or the result will be fall fruit.

One other item ; the character of the same apple is greatly changed for the better if planted on the mountain. The Limber Twig for instance, which on the mountain is an excellent rosy-cheeked apple, is a green tough apple when planted in the valley.

Pears.

The pear, like the apple, does not do well in a hot climate. But few are raised in the southern states. The supply is brought from the north and from California. They are sold by retail at from five to ten cents each. On the Cumberland lands pears will do well if planted in deep, good soil, and especially if planted on the north side or on the top of the hills. The market will always be unlimited in the south, especially for good winter pears.

Winter varieties and standard trees are recommended. Dwarf trees might be planted between the rows of standards, and thus economise space. The dwarfs will be nearly worn out by the time the standards are in full bearing. If the dwarfs are planted four inches below the point of union with the quince-stock, it will often become a standard by throwing out lateral roots.

The following varieties were selected from one
hundred specimens of fruit from Ellwanger and
Bang's, Rochester, N.Y., and are known from trial
to be of first quality, and to do well in this climate :—
namely, Bartlett, Buffin, Kirtland Seckel, Jalonisa
d'Fonteney, Duchess d'Anguleme (splendid), Louise
Bonne de Jersey, Vicar of Wakefield (excellent for
winter), Howell, Belle Lucrative, Beurre de Aangore,
Seckel, Tyson, Sheldon, Beurre Bosc, Beurre Gifford
(very early), Bellflowet, Beurre Diel, Clairgeau, Clapp's
Favourite, Swan's Orange.   Of these the Duchesse,
Vicar of Wakefield, Belle Lucrative, Howell, Sheldon,
Beurre Bosc, Beurre Gifford, Clapp's Favourite, and
Swan's Orange are unsurpassed.   Most of the above
list are summer and fall pears.

It is believed that quinces, cherries, plums, and
nectarines will all do well at Rugby.

Grapes.

Grapes, when planted in deep soil, where the rock
does not approach too near the surface, unquestionably
will do well on the table-land.   The porosity of the
soil in many places, and the absence of a heavy clay
subsoil, secure for the roots of the vine, a dry, healthy
bed, and thus prevent rot and mildew, the great enemy
of the grape vine in heavy clay soils.   Grapes require
a rich, deep, loose, porous soil.   Such places may be
found at intervals on the plateau.   It is in vain to
expect a heavy crop of grapes on poor soil.   The vine
will be unthrifty, and the crop from it light.   Fertilise
well with wood ashes, well rotted manure, bone dust,
or ground bone, or something of the kind, or one need
not expect healthy vigorous vines, and good crops on

poor land. Without these, one may as well expect a
heavy crop of corn on poor land.

If grapes are raised for market, Cincinnati will be
the best point for the early, and the southern cities
for the late. At Chattanooga and Knoxville, the
season being early and hot, the latest grapes are
generally ripe and exhausted by the 20th, or at least
by the last of September. There is always a demand
for more after the home supply is exhausted. This is
supplied by grapes from Lake Erie.

The season at Rugby, owing to its elevated situation, is ten or fifteen days later than in the valley
south of it. The result will be that late grapes at
Rugby will just be maturing as they are disappearing
at Chattanooga and Knoxville. If a good grape can
be found, which will mature in October, and if it can
be preserved in a good state until November or
December, there will always be a demand for such a
grape in the southern cities. The following varieties
are recommended after trial. Early, Eumelan (excellent and certain), Medium, Concord, and Ives Seedling; Late, Catawba (for wine), Concord, Norton's
Virginia, and Ives Seedling.

It may be well to add that the grapes grown on
the Cumberland plateau have a thicker skin than
those grown in the valley, and will bear transportation
much better. They will also keep longer in a sweet
condition.

Strawberries.

Strawberries will mature ten days later at Rugby
than at Knoxville and Chattanooga. They will no
doubt mature there a few days before they will at

Cincinnati. If so, that will be the place for early marketing. For the late crop, the cities south of Rugby. The last strawberries, if good, always sell high and readily. People never grow tired of them if good.

Splendid strawberries can be raised at Rugby. The sandy soil and climate both suit them. They need and require rich food, such as a heavy coat of stable manure, wood ashes, ground bone, plaster, phosphates, etc. The ground cannot be made too rich for them.

The following varieties have all been fully tested, and are recommended : — Early, Metcalf's early, Downer's Prolific, Barne's Mammoth, Monarch of the West (the last of huge size). Main crop, Charles Downing, Boyden's No. 30, Agriculturist, Jucunda, and Monarch of the West. Late, Kentucky.

Raspberries.

These will do well on the table-lands. All the red varieties are natives of a cold climate. They are the most productive and delicate in taste. They require very rich and deep soil. After the trial of many varieties, the writer recommends the Hudson River Antwerp as the hardiest and best variety. It is perfectly hardy in this climate, standing both heat and cold better than any other. A later kind, if one could be found, would be very valuable for a late crop.

Peaches.

That there have been peaches of the best quality grown on the mountain cannot be denied by any one who has witnessed the shipments made by Mr. H. N. Caldwell to Nashville a few years ago. The difficulty in raising this fruit comes from the untimely frosts in spring, frequently destroying, or partially destroying two crops in three. A place selected on a northern slope, and a mulching of straw put about the trees when the ground is frozen, will retard inflorescence beyond the period of frosts. By taking this trouble a fine crop of peaches may possibly be grown every year. The writer has often seen peaches three inches in diameter grown on the mountain, and of a lusciousness and juciness unsurpassed by those grown in any country. Seedlings bear oftener than budded fruit. Trees have been known to bear in favourable localities for forty years in succession. One such tree now stands on the mountain above Sherwood, in Franklin county. Careful attention may avert many evils to which the peach tree is subjected.

Cattle Raising.

Cattle raising has always been profitable on the Cumberland plateau. The wild grass which grows so luxuriantly everywhere is sufficient from April till the latter part of November. The Cumberland plateau is a natural pasture. But hay, grass, and roots, such as turnips, vegetables, etc., must be provided for winter. Orchard grass is perhaps the best winter as well as the best summer grass for pasture in this climate. It requires, to do well, rich soil. The north hill-sides, where the soil is richest, will be the best place for it. This grass never runs or dies out if there is a reasonable amount of nourishment in the soil. Cattle are very fond of it. It makes excellent hay also.

A good supply of rough food for cattle can always be had from millet, pea vines, timothy, clover, or red

top.   The new system of saving green food for stock,
termed *ensilage*, can be most profitably adopted.   For
the method of saving and curing green food under this
system, refer to the report of Professor J. M. M'Bride,
of the University of Tennessee, at Knoxville.   Apply
to him for said report.

In the low places described as glades often grows a
rough grass (*Panicum crusgalli*), known as bear grass,
which supplies a great deal of food to cattle.   Beggars'
lice (*Lynoglossum Morisoni*) abounds on the mountain,
and furnishes a very nutritious food to cattle.   In fact
they grow fat upon it.

Sheep Raising.

It has always been asserted and believed that sheep
raising can be as cheaply done on the Cumberland
plateau as in any part of the United States, possibly
excepting Texas, Colorado, and New Mexico.   In the
northern states, where the winters are much longer and
more severe, sheep raising is very profitable.   Why
should it not be so here, with unlimited natural pasturage so many months in the year? and it is said, but
the writer is not certain of the fact, that good spring
lambs are worth about five dollars each in Cincinnati.
Certainly every farmer can add largely to his income
by having a flock of the best varieties of sheep for wool
and mutton, and a ready market can always be had in
Cincinnati.   Care must be taken, however, to have
them sheltered during the stormy weather of winter.
Pea haulm or clover hay should also be provided for
them.   During the summer months they can live upon
the wild grasses and do well, but these grasses must
not be relied upon to keep them through the winter.

Tobacco.

Unquestionably a very fine manufacturing leaf may be grown upon the mountain. It has frequently been done. If the White Burley, cured without fire, were planted and well cured, it would form the basis for extensive plug manufacturing upon the mountain. There is no more profitable employment in the United States than the manufacture of a type of tobacco suitable for American consumption. In addition to this variety, seed leaf for wrappers and Cuba for fillers could be very profitably grown and worked up into cigars. The most thriving farming communities in America are those in which tobacco is grown for consumption in America. The great mistake made in many southern states is that the farmers have grown tobacco for exportation, and neglected their best customers at home. No crop in proportion to value is more easily grown.

Pea-Nuts, or the Ground Pea.

The Pea-nut is gradually extending its limits of culture. It is also becoming more and more popular, not only for eating, but for making oil. It likes a loose, friable, partially sandy or gravelly soil, and in colour partakes of the hue of the soil in which it is planted. From forty to sixty bushels per acre may be grown upon the best soils of the table-land, and, as one man can take care of eight acres, the raising of the crop will be fairly remunerative. The price fluctuates very much, sometimes being as high as one dollar per bushel, and then falling to sixty cents. Cincinnati is the great market for the pea-nut, and the colonists

would always find a ready sale for this product.
There are two varieties grown—the white and the red.
The former is planted in hills three feet apart, the
latter in drills the same distance.   Level culture is
best for this crop.

Lima Beans and Navy Beans.

Lima beans and navy beans can be grown with great
success on the mountain.   The yield can be made to
reach from one hundred to one hundred and fifty
bushels per acre, and with high culture and a good
season the yield can be made two hundred bushels.
The cultivation of these will be found as remunerative
as any crop that can be planted.   Corn-field peas will
also pay well.   When boiled or ground into meal
they are excellent for stock.   No food will cause cows
to give richer milk than pea meal.   It should be
mixed with corn meal or wheat bran.

Manufactures.

There is no good reason why certain kinds of manufactures should not be successful at Rugby, or near it, on
the Cincinnati Southern Railroad ; such, for example, as
iron furnaces, tanneries, furniture, boots and shoes,
waggon and carriage factories; and factories for making
spokes, hubs, handles, and many others of a similar
character.

As for iron, it is a well-known fact that pig-iron can
be manufactured in portions of Tennessee, Georgia, and
Alabama, at a cost from $5 to $7 per ton less than at
Pittsburg, or Hanging Rock, Ohio.   This is owing to
the close juxtaposition of coal, iron ore, and limestone,
and the cheapness of labour and provisions, but chiefly

the former.   A margin of profit of $5 a ton will pay a remarkable dividend.   Coal of the best quality is found on the Cumberland Plateau, and iron ore and limestone in the lower valleys.

Tanneries also ought to yield a good profit.   The Cumberland Plateau abounds in Chestnut Oak, the bark of which is in great demand in tanning.   This bark is now being shipped to Cincinnati.   If it will pay to ship the bark a long distance, it ought to pay much better to bring the lighter article (the hides) to the place where the bark can be found.   Labour, rents, and provisions, would be cheaper at Rugby than in a large city.   It seems that no point would be better for a steam tannery than this.

Factories for making furniture, especially the cheap furniture, such as is made out of poplar, walnut, and pine, should also pay well, if economically and skilfully managed.   These woods everywhere abound on the plateau.   Vast quantities of walnut are daily shipped from there to New York and Boston, much of which returns in the shape of fine furniture.

In the southern states, among the coloured race, there is a constant demand for cheap furniture, such as tables, bedsteads, etc.   Fine furniture is also in demand. Most of this is at present manufactured in New York and Cincinnati, much of it out of Tennessee walnut, and transported to the south at a heavy cost, and sold at a high profit.   This double cost of transportation would afford a wide margin of profit, to say nothing of anything else.

As for all articles made out of white oak and hickory, such as waggons, carriages, spokes, hubs, handles, etc. etc., it seems that some point on the

plateau would combine every element for their successful manufacture.   The forests are full of the very
best white oak and hickory.   They grow all along the
railroad.   A lumber dealer from the city of New York
recently remarked that the white oak timber of East
Tennessee was the best in the world.   Hence lumber
dealers and manufacturers from a distance are seeking
for it, as they are for our walnut.

We have thus attempted to give some idea of the
capability and adaptation of the soil of Rugby to the
different kinds of crops, grasses, and fruits ; to point
out the most profitable pursuits ; the best mode of
culture ; and to call attention to the facilities which
exist for profitable manufacturing enterprises.   We
admit the imperfectness of our attempt.   But we believe there has been no overcolouring, and certainly no
intentional misrepresentation.   We hope that our work
may in some degree serve to keep those who are un-
familiar with the climate, soil, and products of the
plateau, from falling into great errors and mistakes.
We are sure that those who follow our advice will not
be so likely to do so.

We venture one other suggestion.   Let those who
intend farming, in the larger sense of the term, as well
as those who intend to follow market gardening or
fruit raising, *not risk all on one crop or article, but
let them diversify their products,* so that if one fails
others may succeed.

Colonists should not be discouraged by the opinions
of the farmers of the south, for the reason that the
latter have yet to learn the value of manures.   Accustomed through generations to work nothing else but
virgin soils which require no adventitious aid, they

cannot understand how the thin soils of the Cumberland plateau can ever be profitably cultivated. But
if one such farmer should visit the sand blows of
Connecticut where, by the application of ten cords of
manure, a profit of $300 per acre is often realised, he
could begin to understand that even poverty of soil
may be overcome by care and labour. And the history
of agriculture in America demonstrates the fact that
rich soils alone are no guarantee of future growth and
prosperity. Oftentimes the very fertility of the soil
breaks up those habits of systematic industry which
lie at the very foundation of all permanent progress.
That the Cumberland plateau, from its salubrity, its
accessibility to markets, its adaptability to fruits and
vegetables, its wealth of coal and timber, will in time
become a populous region, there can be no doubt. It
should always be remembered, however, that patient
labour, guided by skill and intelligence, is positively
necessary to make agriculture profitable.

With these, the prediction of Andrew Jackson may
be verified that it will become the Garden of Tennessee.

GLOSSARY.

A.

ALIENS, Rights of, in Tenn.
    Same as those of citizens, without electoral vote.
ALLEGHANY CHAIN, Distance to.
    80 or 90 miles.
ASSISTANCE offered by Board, wherein consisting ?
    PUBLIC WORKS.
        Deferred payments for land, forwarding settlers by agent from
        New York.
        Advice from Company's gardener and forester, and officials, etc.
        etc.
    (*See* Credit given by the Board.)

B.

BACON, Price at Settlement.
    11c. per lb.   5½d.
BEEF, Price at Settlement.
    5c. to 10c. per lb.   2½d. to 5d.
BUTTER, Price at Settlement.
    25c. per lb.   1s. 0½d.
BEE-KEEPING, Information as to.
    Bees do very well.
BOARDING-HOUSES, What existing ?
    1. Otis Brown.
    2. Thos. Grooms.
    3. Mrs. O'Connor (board only).
    4. Tim. Galloway (board only).
    5. "Barracks" (board and lodging).
BOARD OF AID, etc., Scope and Purpose of.
    (*See* Body of Pamphlet, President's Address, etc.)
BRICKS, Price at Settlement.
        $7.00 per thousand.   £1 : 9 : 2.

M

C.

CAPITAL, Amount required by Settlers.

Those with a family should have from $1000 to $2000. £200 to £400.

CARPENTERS, Wages at Settlement.

$1.50 to $2.25 per day. 6s. 3d. to 9s. 4d.

CATTLE, Price at Settlement.

2 years old in spring, $7.00 to $10.00. £1 : 9 : 2 to £2 : 1 : 6. Draught oxen, $50 to $75 per pair. £10 : 5s. to £15 : 10s.

CHURCH ACCOMMODATION, What existing?

One Church Building, Church of England Service on Sundays. Presbyterian and other Services, occasionally.

CLIMATE, Maximum and Minimum temperature, snow, drought and floods.

Highest summer temperature, about 97°. Lowest winter temperature, —7°. Average summer temperature, 71°. Average winter temperature, about 35°. Snow only lies a few days in winter. Rainfall estimated at about 50. Rivers often in flood, but do not reach cultivated lands.

COAL, Obtainable for fuel.—No mines as yet open.

Large deposits within short distance of Settlement.

COFFEE, Price at Settlement.

20c. per lb. 10d.

COLONISTS, What classes at Settlement?

Officials, artisans, agricultural and other settlers.

(*See* also :—Residents.)

—— What classes expected?

Agricultural and residential.

COMMISSARY, Store.

Five dollar shares (= £1) can be taken by settlers, entitling them to share of profits in proportion to the amount of their purchases.

CORN CROPS, Prospect of.

Healthy, but not a heavy yield.

CORN, Price at Settlement.

50c. per bushel. 2s. 1d.

CREDIT given by Board.

Country lots :—One-fourth cash ; one-fourth end of the second year ; one-fourth end of the third year ; balance end of the fourth year. Interest six per cent. Town lots, no credit.

D.

DRAINAGE OF TOWN, System to be adopted.
    A plan has been submitted by an eminent medical authority,
        which is being put in force.
DWELLING-HOUSES, Any to rent?
    Houses being built.

E.

EMPLOYMENT, Temporary, for Immigrants.   Does Board find any?
    Board cannot guarantee it.
—— OF SETTLERS.   What branches most remunerative?
    Gardening, small farming, and stock-raising.

F.

FARES by American Steamship Company of Philadelphia, 17 Water
    Street, Liverpool. *Liverpool to Sedgemoor, via Philadelphia*—
    Cabin, £15 : 15s. to £21 ; Intermediate, £11 : 8 : 3 ; Steerage,
    £8 : 10 : 10.   By other routes, railway fare from New York to
    Sedgemoor, about $16.
FIREWOOD, Price at Settlement.
    $1.00 per cord, 4 feet long, delivered.   4s. 2d.
FLOUR, Price at Settlement.
    $5.00 to $7.00 per bbl.   21s. to 29s.
FRUIT-GROWING, Prospects of.
    Very good ; large and certain market.
FURNITURE, Purchaseable on spot?
    Can be bought in Cincinnati, or can be ordered through the
    Commissary.

G.

GAME, What kinds?

Bear (seen occasionally).	Rabbits.
Deer (fairly numerous).	Raccoon.
Turkey (fairly numerous).	Opossum.
Wood Grouse (common).	Fish (Bass, Pike small).
Quail (common).	Squirrels (common).
Duck (occasional).	

GARDENING, Prospects of.

Very good.

GRASS, Green all the year?

Good growth of winter grass, but stock require feeding during part of most winters.

GRASSES OF THE PLATEAU.

Sedge luxurious in the spring, and excellent early food, followed by a good growth of the southern winter grasses, and a variety of herbs and shrubs furnish good feed as well. Orchard and red-top, as well as clovers, will repay cultivation. Bermuda is worthy of trial.

H.

HAULING, Can it be hired?

Horse, team, and driver, $2.50 per day. 10s. 6d.

Oxen, team, and driver, $2.75. 11s. 6d.

HAY CROP, Prospect of.

Clover, millet, and rye yield heavy crops.

HELP, Female, Cost at Settlement.

Scarce: $6.00 to $10.00 per month. 25s. to 41s. 8d.

HERD, Information as to.

Board contemplate organising one.

(*See* President's Address, p. 120).

HOGS, Price at Settlement.

Very cheap.

HORSES, Price at Settlement.

$60 to $125. £12 : 10s. to £26.

—— How fed in winter?

Corn, millet, hay, etc.

HORSE-FEED, Price at Settlement?

Corn, 50c. per bushel, 2s. 1d.; Hay, $20 per ton, £4 : 3 : 4, varying with the season.

HOTEL, Any at Settlement?

Tabard Hotel, first-class, but limited accommodation $2 a day. 8s. 4d., or $30 a month.

HOUSES, Cost of to build.

Four rooms, $300 (= say £62): others in proportion.

HOUSEHOLD UTENSILS.

To be obtained at Commissary.

HUNTSVILLE, Population, and how many stores?

Population about 100 ; several stores.

I.

IMPROVEMENTS, Does Board allow for?

No leases granted at present, but the point will be considered should occasion arise.

INTEREST CHARGED BY BOARD.

Six per cent on deferred payments.

J.

JAMESTOWN, Population of, and how many stores?

Population, about 100 ; two stores.

L.

LIQUOR, Restrictions on sale of.

Manufacture and Sale positively prohibited.

LUMBER, Price at Company's saw mill.

$14 per thousand, delivered on town site ; price liable to revision. £2 : 18 : 4.

LABOUR, Household and field, male and female. Cost of.

Male, $1.00 per day, without board. 4s. 2d.

Female, $2.00 per week, with board. (See "Help" above.) 8s. 4d.

Coloured or white? Both.

LANDS, Cost of?

Farm lands, $5.00 to $10.00 per acre. 20s. 10d. to 41s. 8d.

Description of—hilly or flat? etc.

Mostly undulating plateau, with deep gorges.

On or near new road—price of?

$6.00 to $10.00 per acre. 25s. to 41s. 8d.

Who will show?

Officers of the Board at Rugby.

M.

MALARIA, Any in region?

None.

MANUFACTURES.

None as yet established.

MAPS OF REGION, What published?

Map of Tennessee Colton, New York.

Map of Tennessee, Killebrew, Nashville.

Plan of town site, by Board, and other surveys in progress.

MARKET, Nearest for grain, cattle, sheep, etc.
　　　Cincinnati and Kentucky towns.
　　　Chattanooga and the South.
MILCH COWS, Price at Settlement.
　　　$15 to $30.　£3 : 2 : 6 to £6 : 5s.
MOSQUITOES ?·
　　　None.
MUTTON, 5c. to 10c. per lb.　2½d. to 5d.

O.

OXEN, Draught, Price at Settlement.
　　(*See* Cattle).

P.

PASTURE, Character of.
　　　Natural grass good in spring and summer ; moderate in winter.
　　　　Will be much improved by sowing.
PLANS OF LANDS FOR SALE.
　　　Surveys in Progress.　Plans will be shown at Rugby by Board's
　　　　Surveyor, and at London Office.
PLOUGHS, Price at Settlement.
　　　Common, $6.00 to $8.00.　25s. to 33s. 4d.
POST-OFFICE, Information as to.
　　　Post-Office at Rugby.　Letters can be registered, but money
　　　　orders are not yet issued.
POULTRY, Price at Settlement.
　　　About 12c. apiece.　6d.
PROFESSIONAL Men, Opening for.
　　　Filled up at present.

R.

RECOMMENDATIONS, Any required ?
　　　None ; but it would be well for persons seeking employment to
　　　　bring some credentials.
RESIDENTS AT SETTLEMENT.
　　　Many sites have been already selected for residences of families
　　　　wishing for a climate mild as compared with Northern winters,
　　　　and never oppressively hot in summer.
ROAD TO RAILROAD, Any made ?
　　　Good road, 6¾ miles to Sedgemoor Station.

ROBBINS, Where located ?

    8 miles east from Rugby ; 219 miles from Cincinnati.

RULES AND REGULATIONS to be enforced.

    Liquor selling prohibited ; other points left to public feeling.

RUNNING WATER, Supply of on lands.

    Abundant and unfailing supply from mountain streams ; above
    level of streams supply from wells uncertain.

S.

STOREHOUSES, Any to be rented ?

    None.

STORE-KEEPER, Any opening for ?

    Not at present.

SUGAR, Price at Settlement.

    9c to 12c per lb.   4½d. to 6d.

SNAKES, Any ?

    Yes, but not troublesome.

SOIL OF BOARD-LANDS, Nature of.

    Sandy loams and clay.

SOUTHERN SUSCEPTIBILITIES, Are they likely to cause trouble ?

    No.

STOCK-FARMING, Prospects of.

    Pronounced good by independent experts.

STONE, Building, Supply at Settlement.

    Excellent building stone close to town site.

SANITARY CONDITION OF REGION.

    Region remarkably healthy.

SCHOOL ACCOMMODATION, What existing ?

    Board school in course of erection.

SEDGEMOOR, Station on Cincinnati Southern Railway.

    6¾ miles from settlement ; 221 miles from Cincinnati.

SETTLEMENT, Present population.

    May 1881, between 250 and 300.

SHEEP-FARMING LANDS, Price, and how situated to town ?

    $4.00 to $6 00 ; within a ten-mile radius. 16s. 8d. to 25s.

SKUNKS, Any ?

    Yes : called pole-cats.

T.

TAXATION, State.

    30c. on $100 at present (= 6s. per cent).

  ,,   Local, never exceeds State tax.

TEAMS, Cost at Settlement.
> (*See* Waggons, Horses, Oxen).

TENNESSEE, State Laws of.
> Liberal to aliens.

TERMS OF PAYMENT FOR LANDS.
> (*See* Credit).

TIMBER, Where ? How much ?
> On all lands except where cleared.   Not much under-brush.

TITLES, Tennessee, State of ;
> Generally complicated ; but Board titles guaranteed.

TOWNS IN VICINITY, and population.
> Huntsville, population 100, county seat, Scott county, distant 14 miles.
> Jamestown, population 100, county seat, Fentress county, distant 18 miles.
> Wartburg, population 300, county seat, Morgan county, distant 22 miles.

V.

VEGETABLE RAISING, Prospects of.
> Very good.

W.

WAGES, in Settlement.
> Labourers, 50c. per day, and board.   2s. 1d.
> Labourers, $1.00 per day, without board.   4s. 2d.

WAGGONS, Prices.
> $60 to $100.   £12 : 10s. to £20 : 16 : 8d.

WATER, At what depth ?
> Springs and streams in abundance ; a 30-ft. well will strike water almost anywhere.

WOOD-CUTTING, Can it be hired ?
> $1.00 per day.   4s. 2d.